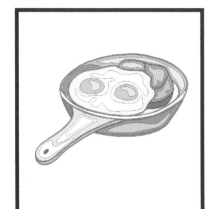 EL DESAYUNO

 El MACHETE

 El TOMATE

 El TENEDOR

 LA ESPÁTULA

 LAS BEBIDAS

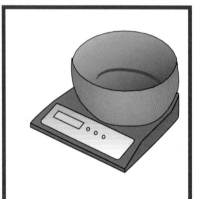 LA BÁSCULA

 El TAZÓN

 LOS HUEVOS

 LAS ZANAHORIAS

 LA CUCHARA

 LA ENSALDA

Latin Lover Lite

Chef LaLa

Spencer Publications

USA

SPENCER PUBLICATIONS
5737 Kanan Road # 215
Agoura Hills, CA 91301

For information regarding discounts for bulk purchases
Please contact Spencer Publications at 818-991-1572
jsbmanagement@aol.com

Designed by Chef LaLa
Graphics and Layout

Cover Graphics: Sean Tatalovich

Printed in China by Regal Printing

Library of Congress Cataloging-in Publication Data

ISBN 0-9760417-0-7

Recipes, Styling and Text: Chef LaLa

Photography: Stephen Anderson

Location Photography: Chef LaLa

Contents

FORWARD

It wasn't long ago that mothers would call their young daughters into the kitchen to help prepare the next meal. During these times women would talk, share ideas and dice "las verduras" (veggie ingredients). Mothers wanted to ensure that their daughters knew how to prepare their husband's meal when their daughters were married. So year after year, daughters took note of the recipes and techniques. Most recipes were not written down. Recipes were often memorized, and handed down generation to generation.

Along the way, husbands and sons also took note of the ingredients and today men often prepare some of the best meals for modern day families. But times have changed and in an era of working parents, drive through restaurants, cell phones and satellite e-mail, the art of preparing, "cosinando"- a meal is all but gone. The irony is that in today's reality, the time we take to prepare a meal has become a luxury. Today everyone is focused on low carbohydrate diets and eating as quickly as time permits.

It is no wonder we have seen such a resurgence and fascination for cooking and to see the kitchen as a studio for producing gastronomic art! Today we find the kitchen is a place we can take charge of, it is place of experimentation, creativity and innovation. Men as well as women own the kitchen. Many men claim the eight-burner stove with dual convection ovens as "their toy". Equally as important, women find they are no longer in the kitchen to entice their future husbands' cravings but rather because they can find enchantment in the kitchen, without judgment or fear of chastisement from peers. They can just create or they can refer to this book for inspiration. Passion for our culture and a deep desire to ensure that our children and families experience the flavor, color and richness of Latin America's dishes will make this book indispensable.

In the kitchen the often-dulled senses are rekindled and the imagination breaks boundaries. Risking the blemish of the salsa on the work suit we can recreate a taste from a perfect memory embedded in the taste buds. For many in today's world, perfection is the goal, designer kitchens and homes. But the truth is a perfect kitchen does not create a perfect meal. It is that chance spice, that nontraditional combination of fruit and vegetables that becomes magic and communal. It was in this spirit that mole must have been created. Imagine chocolate and peanut butter with crushed red chilies or sweet plantains with black beans or jicama with chili...the only way these ingredients could have come together is through the magic of experimentation. And truth be told, it's not like combining two explosives with the potential of blowing up the kitchen! Combining foods with just the right spices, eaten just at the right time and sharing the bounties with family and friends is probably one of life's most satisfying moments.

Our world moves so fast, there is little time to reflect upon those things that really matter. Some people can profess that we should eat to live and not live to eat. These people have not fully lived. When we think about our lives, most people will remember their children, their loved ones, places traveled or not traveled; they will also remember a tune, singing, dancing and yes, a certain aroma of what was an epicurean delight. Your taste buds will take you back home, if only momentarily but what a wonderful visit.

Imagine for a moment a world without food. It is not possible. Therefore, we should enjoy not just the food, but the taste, the look, the colors, the people around us as we share the food, the experimentation in the kitchen of spices and liquids and everything else that comes with the magic of creation. And if you follow the recipes in this book, the magic will be that much better because it will be guilt free..."provecho".

Gisselle Acevedo-Franco
President and General Manager
HOY, Los Angeles

"There is no love sincerer than the love of food."

-George Bernard Shaw (1856-1950)

For most of my life I have struggled with my weight. As one of the more than 60 percent of adults in the United States who are obese or overweight, I tried just about everything to shed pounds—and even succeeded at times—only to watch the numbers on the scale climb back up again. Over the years I've taken metabolic enhancers and fat blockers. I've attempted detox, vegetables-only and high-protein diets. I even went on the 48-Hour Diet for 96 hours. Each time, I quickly tired of all the rules about what you could and couldn't eat. I felt deprived and my energy level inevitably bottomed out. What was worse was that I longed for flavorful food.

It's no surprise that no matter what gimmick or plan I tried, I couldn't stick with it; the weight always came back. At one point, a doctor friend told me, "It's in your genes, and unless a pill is invented to change the make-up of your family genetics, I am afraid you are going to have to work harder." I began to think that the only thing that would change would be my *jeans* from time to time because of the constant weight loss and gain.

Frankly, I should have known better. After all, I am a nutritionist. But I am also a chef, and I'm passionate about food. My love affair with food was one of the reasons I became a chef. From childhood I was seduced by the decadent flavors and textures of Latin dishes, especially my family's native Mexican cuisine. I wanted to continue to fulfill this passion, but at the same time I needed to put an end to my yo-yo dieting. What I wanted more than anything was to enjoy food while also feeling sexy, energetic and fabulous. I had to find a happy—and healthy—medium.

There were plenty of obstacles to achieving that goal. First, I've always hated bland food. Whenever I'm in the kitchen or at the table, the Latina in me kicks in and I NEED FLAVOR! In my mind, somewhere, I was conditioned to think good for you = rice cakes. No gracias!

My other big problem was finding time to eat regular meals. Between family, filming, traveling, recipe development, catering, community service, television appearances and writing a book, I rarely made the time to exercise or to prepare a well-balanced meal for myself. And as a chef, I often lost my appetite when I was in the kitchen for too long no matter how good the food was. Other times—like many of you—I just got so busy with work that I'd forget to eat at a set time.

Filming at
MADRES Restaurant
Pasadena, California

I could fill a meat locker with all the excuses I've made for not eating a healthy and balanced diet. When I was unhappy about how I looked on television or in a picture, I would say, "No one trusts a skinny chef." Maybe that's true, but it was little consolation. My body and soul still didn't feel right.

The fact is that what we eat plays a role in our health, appearance, performance and well-being. As a health professional, I knew I needed to take the frustration and deprivation out of weight management, and allow myself to adopt gradual, realistic changes that would make healthy eating and physical activity a permanent pleasure.

That's not always easy to do, especially with all of the conflicting information that exists about weight loss and diets. You could spend a lifetime studying all of the nutritional data that exists. Even I had information overload: What is good for you and what isn't? How many hours does it take to burn off carbohydrates versus proteins? It's exhausting to apply every single rule, and often, the rules are contradictory.

Here are some simple truths that I've learned through my work as a nutritionist, my success as a chef and my failure as a dieter:
• It's difficult to keep your weight in check when you're depriving yourself. Keep in mind that the human body took shape millions of years ago, and the only low-calorie event in people's lives was starvation. Those who could cope with a temporary lack of food were the ones who survived. Our bodies, therefore, have developed a built-in mechanism that helps us survive when the food supply is low. Eating less than 1,200 calories a day usually is not enough to support a basal metabolism, so your body will compensate by burning less energy. (In other words, it's storing calories instead of using them.)

Also, skipping meals makes you more likely to make up for those missing calories by snacking or eating more at your next meal. The best approach is to eat four to five smaller meals rather than two to three big ones. This averts hunger and trains you to eat less per sitting.

• People who diet without exercising often get fatter with time. Although your weight might drop initially when dieting, you're losing mostly water and muscle. When the weight returns, it comes back as fat. To avoid gaining fat over time, you should increase your metabolism by exercising regularly. Choose an exercise routine that you are comfortable with. It should be something that strengthens your bones and tones your muscles while helping you to control your weight.

• Good-tasting food doesn't have to be fattening or complicated to create. Latin cuisine is exhilarating and it's exotic, and with ingredients increasingly available at your neighborhood grocery store, it's easier to make than ever before. I've taken age-old Latin recipes passed down through generations of my family (as well as dishes I've discovered as a chef and in my travels throughout Latin America) and combined them with my formal culinary training and nutritional expertise to create a healthy meal plan. The result is food with more color, flavor, texture and aroma than even I imagined was possible.

While most of us recognize the need to eat healthier foods, it is difficult to translate the recommended guidelines into enticing, wholesome meals. I wanted this cookbook to be realistic for today's busy person, with recipes that are not too time-consuming or hard to follow. Throughout the book I also explain the basics about proteins, carbohydrates, fat, calories, salt and water so you can feel confident that you're making the best possible food choices.

What you won't find in this book are watered-down versions of Latin classics. On the contrary, these are authentic, full-flavored foods that also happen to be good for you. Stuffed peppers, marinated steaks, black bean soup, plantains—these all can be prepared in traditional ways that are surprisingly healthy.

I once read somewhere the following quote and it has stayed with me ever since: "No one can give us wisdom. We must discover it for ourselves on the journey through life, which no one can take for us." That has been so true in my own experience. Once I recognized what I call "my bads"—not taking time to eat properly, making excuses for my weight, choosing unhealthy foods, failing to exercise—it became easier to correct my mistakes. I realized that it wasn't my weight or dress size that was important, but how I felt. I wanted to feel healthy and energetic, not deprived and angry because I was on a diet, or overweight and sluggish because I wasn't exercising or making good food choices.

Learning from your mistakes is the best way to institute permanent change. Behaviorists say that in order to achieve our goals we must learn as we go. This means that with each step we get closer and closer to the desired outcome, but only if we learn through our errors. Only you can say, "This is 'my bad.'" Only you know the whole truth. Only you can make a change for the better.

It's also important to keep in mind that we form good habits the same way we form bad ones—through repetition. Once you've begun to institute positive changes in your diet and lifestyle, you can make them a part of your routine. Make daily commitments to yourself (for instance, making time to eat a well-balanced lunch or dinner), and keep those commitments whether you feel like it or not. When changing your diet it's important to measure your progress not just by the changes in your appearance, but by the healthy new habits you're adopting.

I wrote this book because I wanted to share with others my struggle with weight maintenance, my nutritional knowledge and my passion for Latin cooking. I hope the information and recipes I've provided will help you navigate your way through the exotic world of Latin cooking without fearing for your waistline. The heavenly aromas and delicious tastes should be reason enough to experiment with these recipes—never mind that the finished dishes are actually good for you.

If you love Latin food, whether you're watching your weight or not, this is the perfect place to start.

Together, let's discover the Latin Lover in you!

calories

Food is fuel. And everyone's body needs this energy, in the form of calories, in order to function.

A calorie measures the amount of energy that nutrients such as protein, carbohydrates and fat supply to your body. Some nutrients have more calories than others:

> One gram of protein = four calories
> One gram of carbohydrates = four calories
> One gram of fat = nine calories

Looking at these numbers, you can see why fat has a such a bad reputation. There are twice as many calories to burn in a gram of fat as there are in a gram of protein or carbohydrates.

There is a simple explanation for why people gain weight: They consume more calories than their bodies need. When you're not burning enough calories through your daily activities, your body stores that unused energy as fat. And for approximately every 3600 calories that you consume but don't use, you gain one pound.

The bottom line is that people become overweight when they eat too much and are not active enough. Most dieticians will tell you that there are no unhealthy foods, only unhealthy diets. Healthy eating is about consuming the right quantity and balance of foods at all times. It's not about whether you succumb to carnitas and flan once in a while. Getting a good balance of nutrients from all the major food groups is the foundation of day-to-day well being, and will reduce your long-term risk of disease.

Moderation is key, both when consuming calories and excluding them. When you go on a low-calorie diet, your body thinks it is starving; it actually becomes more efficient at storing fat by slowing your metabolism. When you stop this unrealistic eating plan, your metabolism remains so slow and inefficient that you gain the weight back even faster, even if you continue to eat less than you did before you began dieting.

Strict, low-calorie diets cause you to lose both muscle and fat in equal amounts. But when you eventually gain back the weight, it will be all fat and not muscle, causing your metabolism to slow down even more. These diets are simply too restrictive to promote healthy weight loss. More likely than not, by following one of these diets you'll eventually end up with extra weight, a less-healthy body composition and a less-attractive physique.

Of course you should watch your total calorie consumption, but it's more important to know what balance of foods you need to stay healthy. You can—and should—incorporate a variety of foods into your daily routine. And you can do it without skimping on dishes you're sure to enjoy.

protein

It's easy to get the protein your body needs. Protein is found in foods such as meat, chicken, fish, eggs and nuts. Dairy products like cheese, milk and yogurt are also great sources of protein, as are beans, lentils and peas. All animal- and plant-derived foods contain some protein. While the proteins provided by animal sources are closest to those our bodies require, a balanced vegetarian diet also provides adequate protein.

Why do you need protein? For one thing, it builds and repairs body tissues and structures. Your muscles, organs— even some of your hormones—consist mainly of protein. Protein assists the body in other ways, as well. For instance, it is necessary for the production of both hemoglobin (which transports oxygen throughout your body) and antibodies (which help you fight disease and infection).

Protein also provides you with crucial substances that your body is unable to produce on its own. Once in your system, protein breaks down into 20 essential and non-essential amino acids. It is the eight essential amino acids that your body can obtain only from food, and which help to regulate many of your bodily functions, including sleep.

Protein should represent about 15 percent of your daily caloric intake. If you eat too little, your body can't function properly. But eating too much can be just as dangerous. Excess protein forces your kidneys to work harder to eliminate the waste. And chronic consumption of a high-protein diet is associated with a higher intake of saturated fat and a lower intake of fiber, which can put you at risk for heart disease and some types of cancer.

Also bear in mind that when you eat more protein calories than your body needs, they can be stored as fat. Since many of us overconsume protein, it's not surprising that this otherwise essential nutrient contributes to our fat stores. It makes sense then to choose protein-rich foods that also are low in fat.

The ultimate goal is to satisfy the majority of your energy needs with carbohydrates and fat (in moderation, of course), saving protein for tissue repair and growth. This is why carbohydrates are often referred to as "protein sparing." If you do not eat adequate amounts of carbohydrates and/or fats, more protein will be used for energy by default.

If you do choose a diet high in proteins, either as part of a weight-loss plan or to build muscle, be sure to drink lots of water. The more proteins you consume, the more fluids your body needs. To metabolize proteins, your body requires approximately seven times the amount of water that it does to process carbohydrates or fats

carbohydrates

Carbohydrates, which are sometimes called carbs or carbos, are a chief source of energy for all of your body's functions. Since your body requires constant energy to perform, it continually craves this macro nutrient. Carbohydrates also help to regulate the digestion and utilization of protein and fat.

The principal carbohydrates present in food are simple sugars, starches and cellulose. Simple sugars, or glucose, are found primarily in honey and fruits and are easily digested. Double sugars, such as table sugar, require some extra digestive action. Starches, especially those found in whole grains, are far more complex and require prolonged digestion in order to be broken down into simple sugars.

Cellulose, commonly found in the skins of fruits and vegetables, works a little bit differently than other carbohydrates. Because it is largely indigestible by humans, it is not used primarily as energy. Instead, it provides the bulk necessary to keep food moving through your digestive system until it is excreted by the body.

Some of the glucose provided by carbohydrates is used as fuel for the brain, nervous system and muscles, while excess glucose is converted into glycogen and stored in the liver and muscles. Any superfluous glycogen is then converted into fat and stored throughout the body as a reserve source of energy. Your body decides to release the power contained in glycogen or fat based on the type of physical activities you perform, and the length of time you continue those activities. If you're running in bursts or doing another brief exercise, your body relies on glycogen for energy. But if you exercise for long periods, your body turns to its energy reserve – body fat.

People on low-carb diets will rave about how much weight they've lost and how quickly. But it's important to remember that weight gain and loss are related to total caloric intake, not the types of foods you eat. When you drop carbohydrate-rich foods from your diet, it is inevitable that your caloric intake will be reduced. For every gram of glucose removed from your glycogen stores, you also lose 2.7 grams of water. This loss of muscle glycogen (including water) can be quite significant in the first week of a low-carbohydrate diet, and can lead to a dramatic weight loss. This is how low-carbohydrate fad diets can promise such quick results. Long-term and permanent weight loss is associated with a realistic eating plan, not one that severely limits or omits this critical food group.

Complex carbohydrates provide your diet with another important essential — fiber. Fruits, whole grains and vegetables are all excellent sources of fiber, and you'll get the greatest benefits by eating at least five portions of fruit and vegetables a day. Higher intakes of dietary fiber are associated with lower incidence of heart disease and certain types of cancer. In addition, fiber helps you feel sated after a meal, improves your intestinal health and regulates your body's absorption of glucose.

There are, of course, bad carbs. Foods high in refined sugar such as table sugar, sugary drinks, cakes, cookies and candy provide "empty calories." This means that apart from the energy the sugar provides, there is often very little else of nutritional value. Sugar also contributes to tooth decay and gum disease, and can cause blood sugar levels to fluctuate excessively. As a result, it is a good idea to limit your sugar intake.

In a healthy and balanced diet, carbohydrates should total between 50 and 70 percent of your daily caloric intake. Be sure that includes at least 25 grams of fiber.

fat

Lipids, or fats, are the most concentrated source of energy in the diet. One gram of fat yields approximately nine calories when oxidized, meaning that it provides your body with more than twice the calories you'd get from a gram of carbohydrate or protein.

Sure, fat can make you fat. But because of this bad reputation, we're often advised not to eat it at all. The truth is that our bodies need some fat to work properly. Fat insulates our bodies from the cold, cushions our organs and provides energy. Some fats comprise hormones that are necessary to regulate body temperature and blood pressure, while others act as carriers for vitamins A, D and E. If you're truly look-conscious, you'll definitely want to consume some fat—it's essential for healthy skin and hair. When choosing fatty foods, it's important to remember that not all fat is created equal. Many of the fats that people consume actually are a combination of saturated and unsaturated fatty acids. Together these substances make up the total fat content in food, but each type has a different effect on the body.

Saturated fat is the worst of the fats. It is known to increase health risks if consumed in large quantities for a long period of time. In particular, it can increase blood cholesterol levels, which can eventually lead to heart disease. Meat, meat products, dairy products and coconut oil contain the greatest amounts of saturated fat. Altogether you should get no more than 10 percent of your total calories each day from saturated fats. Trimming the fat from meat and eating lower-fat versions of dairy foods are great ways to eliminate excess saturated fat from your diet.

Unsaturated fats are divided into two categories, polyunsaturated and monounsaturated, and they are more beneficial to your health. Particularly good are those derived from fish, known as Omega-3 polyunsaturated fatty acids. These may help prevent heart disease by lowering blood cholesterol levels. They also might help to reduce the symptoms of arthritis, other joint problems and certain skin diseases. Good sources of polyunsaturated fats are oily fish (including mackerel, salmon, trout, herring and sardines) and soft polyunsaturated spreads. Other sources include cooking oils such as sunflower, safflower, grape seed and corn.

Monounsaturated fats are thought to be neutral in terms of their effect on health. They generally are found in olives, nuts and avocados. Both monounsaturated and polyunsaturated fatty acids are thought to improve blood cholesterol levels, and are also believed to play a role in the treatment and prevention of heart disease, hypertension, arthritis and cancer.

Speaking of cholesterol, it is another type of fat and is primarily produced by the body in the liver. High levels of cholesterol in the blood increase the risk of heart disease. There are some foods that are high in cholesterol—including eggs and shell fish—though dietary cholesterol does not contribute much to blood cholesterol in most people. Saturated fats have a greater impact on blood cholesterol, so it's more important to reduce these in your diet.

In deciding which fats are best for you, there is one more thing you need to know: During food processing some fats undergo a chemical process called hydrogenation. To "hydrogenate" means to add hydrogen or, in the case of fatty acids, to saturate them. The process changes a liquid oil—naturally high in unsaturated fatty acids—to a more solid and more saturated form. The greater the degree of hydrogenation, the more saturated the fat becomes. Many commercial products (such as cookies, crackers, cakes, French fries, fried onion rings and donuts) contain hydrogenated or partially hydrogenated vegetable oils. Recent studies suggest that these fats might also raise blood cholesterol.

Eating a lot of fat, particularly saturated fat, is simply unhealthy. Whether you're worried about your weight or your risk for disease, it makes sense to reduce your intake of saturated fat, as well as the total fat content of your diet. That means you should get no more than 10 to 30 percent of your daily calories from fat. Higher fat diets are not conducive to successful weight loss or maintenance, and they appear to increase the ease with which your body converts ingested calories to body fat.

water

I cannot tell you how many misconceptions I have heard about water. For instance, you can get the water you need from any beverage, right? Well, there is a difference between pure water and beverages that contain water. While fruit juice, soft drinks, beer, coffee and tea contain water, they also contain substances (like sugars, alcohol or caffeine, for instance) that actually counteract some of water's positive effects.

Water is essential for digestion and metabolism, acting as a medium for various enzymatic and chemical reactions in the body. It carries nutrients and oxygen to the cells through the blood, regulates body temperature and lubricates joints, which is particularly important if you're arthritic, have chronic muscular-skeletal problems or if you exercise frequently.

If you're trying to lose weight, adequate consumption of water is an absolute necessity. The body fat and muscle that break down during weight loss produce wastes that must be eliminated through the kidneys. Water helps your kidneys to remove these wastes.

Studies provide some support for the general recommendation to drink eight glasses of water. For most people that would add a liter or two (the equivalent of four, medium-sized bottles) to their regular water intake. You can expect to burn an extra 100 calories a day by drinking an additional two liters of water above what you normally would consume. If you're dieting, it also helps to drink a big glass of water whenever you feel hungry or right before a meal or snack. The water fills your stomach briefly, makes you feel full and helps you to stop eating sooner.

Be sure to drink water at regular intervals throughout the day and evening. And always check with your physician before significantly increasing your water intake.

salt

My grandmother used to tell us that if we wanted to lose weight we should cut down on salt. And it's true—if you ease up on the shaker you'll probably notice a few pounds difference the next time you step on a scale. The problem is that what you're losing isn't excess body weight, but water weight. That's because table salt is comprised mainly of sodium, a mineral that retains water in the body.

Sodium is essential for the maintenance of human life. Salt controls the amount of water within our bodies and maintains the critical balance between cells and body fluids. It also helps us to move our muscles. About 70 percent of the human body is comprised of water, and one third of that total is found in blood plasma, digestive secretions, and other body fluids not contained within individual cells. By necessity, these fluid substances contain an average of 0.9 parts of dissolved salt.

Having too much sodium (hypernatremia) or too little (hyponatremia) can be detrimental, even fatal. Adequate sodium balance is necessary for transmitting nerve impulses and proper muscle function, and even a slight depletion of this concentration can cause problems. Athletes who compete in long-distance running events in hot, humid conditions are prime candidates to develop hyponatremia. That is why many sports drinks contain sodium.

So how much salt do you really need? The National Academy of Sciences recommends that Americans consume a minimum of 500 milligrams a day to maintain good health. Your individual needs, however, will vary enormously based on your genetic make-up, lifestyle and general health. If you have high blood pressure, for instance, you'll want to limit your sodium intake to control your condition and reduce the risk of heart disease.

While individual requirements vary, most Americans have no trouble reaching their daily minimum. Most of us consume more sodium than we need, especially those of us who eat a lot of processed foods. The kidneys efficiently eliminate this excess sodium in healthy people. Though you should check with your doctor about the amount of sodium that is appropriate for your needs. Never follow someone else's diet; it could be completely wrong for you.

Being informed of what you are purchasing and consuming is essential in making good choices.

Food labels are very helpful, but only if you are able to understand them.

The following guidance is intended to make it easier for you to use nutrition labels to make quick and informed food choices that contribute to a healthy diet.

Product ingredients are also listed on the label and are listed in order of quantity, with the highest quantity ingredient listed first.

Nutrition Facts/Datos de Nutrición

Serving Size/Tamaño por Ración ¼ Cup ¼ taza (60g)
Servings Per Container about 5 / Raciónes por Envase aprox. 5

Amount Per serving/ Cantidad por Ración

Calories/Calorías: 25
Calories from fat/Calorías de Grasa: 10

% Daily Value/% Valor Diario*

Total Fat/Grasa Total 1.5	2%
Sat Fat/Grasa Sat 0 g	0%
Cholesterol/Colesterol 0mg	
Sodium/Sodio 330 mg	14%
Total Carb/Carb. Total 2g	0%
Dietary Fiber/ Fibra Dietética 0g	0%
Sugars/Azúcares 0g	
Protein/Proteinas 0g	0%

Vitamin/Vitamina A 20% • Vitamin/Vitamina C 4%

Calcium/Calcio 0%   •   Iron/Hierro 0%

* Percentage Daily Values are based on a 2,000 calorie diet.

*Los Valores de los porcentajes Diarios estan basados en una dieta de 2,000 calorias.

	Calories	2000	2500
Total Fat	less than	55g	80g
Sat Fat	less than	20g	25g
Cholesterol	less than	800mg	300mg
Sodium	less than	2000mg	2400mg
Total Carbohydrates		340 mg	375 mg
Dietay Fiber		25g	80g

NUTRITION CHART
This portion of the label provides you with guidelines for 2,000 and 2,500-calorie diets. This gives you the estimate goals of the average person. These values do not take into consideration individual requirements.

SERVING SIZE AND Servings PER CONTAINER

The top of the label tells you exactly how much of the product equals one serving size. The line below tells how many Servings are in the container. The example given lists the serving size as ¼ cup and there are 5 Servings in a can. This information is really useful, especially if the serving size exceeds the amount that YOU eat.

CALORIES

This is the amount of calories contained in ONE SERVING. Again remember, a product that lists a low number of calories may have a correspondingly small serving size. Measure your favorite food and compare it with the actual portion size.

CALORIES FROM FAT

This tells how many of the calories in one serving come from fat. For example, this label reads: Calories 25 and Calories from Fat 10. This means that ten of those 25 calories come from fat. The other 15 calories come from either carbohydrates or protein.
From this number, you can calculate the percentage of fat in one serving. Simply take the number if calories from fat (10) and divide it by the total calories listed (25). One serving size of this product contains less than 40% fat.

TOTAL FAT

This tells you how many grams of fat are in one serving.
You can calculate the calories from fat yourself by taking the grams of fat (1.5 , in this case) and multiplying it by 9 (since there are nine calories in one gram of fat). Rule of thumb: for every 100 calories of food, there should be three grams of fat or less. This means 30% or less of the calories will be from fat.

SATURATED FAT, CHOLESTEROL AND SODIUM

The amount of saturated fat is listed below Total Fat. This tells you how many of those fat grams come from saturated fat. This listing, along with the milligrams of cholesterol and the milligrams of sodium are listed for those who need to watch these numbers for health reasons, such as heart disease.

TOTAL CARBOHYDRATE

This number is how many grams of carbohydrate are present in one serving.
To figure out how many calories come from carbohydrates, you would multiply the total grams (2, in this case) by 4 (calories in one gram of carbohydrate).

DIETARY FIBER AND SUGARS

Both of these are carbohydrates. Many people are concerned with these numbers for health reasons.

PROTEIN

This is how much protein is in one serving.
To calculate how many calories come from protein, take the grams of protein (0, in this case) and multiply it by 4 (there are four calories in one gram of protein).

VITAMINS AND MINERALS

These are the percentages of the Recommended Daily Allowance for certain key nutrients present in the product.

% DAILY VALUE GUIDELINES

The percentages listed on the right side of the label are based on a 2,000 calorie diet. These are listed to give you an idea of how much of your daily diet one serving fulfills. For example, this label lists the % Daily Value for Fat as 21%. This means that if you ate 2,000 calories per day, one serving of this food would provide 2% of your recommended fat allowance. Since the amount of fat in your diet depends on the total amount of calories you eat, this varies from person to person.

breakfast

Fruta con Granola

(Fruit & Granola)

BIONICOS

In many Latin countries it is common to eat a small breakfast consisting of coffee, pan (bread) and fruit.

Also, snacking on fresh fruit with chili powder and lemon, or fruit with yogurt or Bionicos (fruit with condensed milk and nuts) throughout the day is common.

INGREDIENTS

1	tablespoon	granola
1	teaspoon	banana chips
1	teaspoon	coconut, shredded
4	ounces	yogurt with fruit, non-fat
1	ounce	strawberries, sliced
1	teaspoon	walnuts, chopped

METHOD

*   Spoon all ingredients into a glass or bowl.

Note: When making your selection for granola, check the fat content, some brands can be significantly higher than others.

NUTRITIONAL GUIDE
PER SERVING

CALORIES	201
FAT (G)	10
SATURATED	4.9
UNSATURATED	5.1
PROTEIN (G)	6.6
CARBOHYDRATES (G)	24.1
FIBER (G)	4.8
CHOLESTEROL (MG)	14
SODIUM (MG)	60

Tortilla Española
(Spanish Tortilla)

INGREDIENTS

6	ounces	potato
½	teaspoon	canola oil
2	stalks	green onions, shredded
5	large	eggs, whites only
1	large	egg
½	teaspoon	salt
¼	teaspoon	pepper

GREEN ONION

These are onions that have small bulbs and long green stalks. They're usually eaten raw, but you can also grill or sauté them.

Other names: scallion, bunching onion, shallot (in Australia), spring onion (in Britain), Chinese onion, stone leek and cibol.

METHOD

* Wash and boil the potatoes until tender. Peel and cut into medium dice.
* Separate five eggs from the egg whites into a mixing bowl.
* Add one whole egg to egg whites.
* Whip the eggs.
* Add salt and pepper, fold over to combine all ingredients.
* Heat the oil in a small nonstick skillet.
* Add onions, and potatoes to skillet.
* Cook until the potatoes are golden brown.
* Add egg mixture.
* Cook for two minutes .
* Transfer to a preheated oven for 8 minutes at 375°.
* Cook until egg is set or firm.
* Allow to cool.
* Slice into wedges and serve.

Note: This dish is served at room temperature.

NUTRITIONAL GUIDE
PER SERVING

CALORIES	130
FAT (G)	2.6
SATURATED	.8
UNSATURATED	1.8
PROTEIN (G)	442
CARBOHYDRATES (G)	12.9
FIBER (G)	1.5
CHOLESTEROL (MG)	10
SODIUM (MG)	442

salsas

Salsa de mi Abuelita
(Grandma's Salsa)

CHILE DE ÁRBOL

Unlike many chiles, these remain bright red even after drying. They're fairly hot. Don't confuse the dried version with the fresh, which goes by the same name.

NUTRITIONAL GUIDE
PER SERVING

CALORIES	29
FAT (G)	.4
SATURATED	0
UNSATURATED	0
PROTEIN (G)	1.3
CARBOHYDRATES (G)	6.3
FIBER (G)	1.2
CHOLESTEROL (MG)	0
SODIUM (MG)	202

INGREDIENTS

8	each	chiles de árbol
½	teaspoon	olive oil
12	ounces	tomato, quartered
2	ounces	onion, peeled and quartered
3	tablespoons	canned tomato puree
½	clove	garlic, peeled
1	teaspoon	salt

METHOD

* In a skillet, add olive oil and roast chiles until brown.
* Transfer to a blender. Add tomatoes, onion, tomato puree, garlic and salt.
* Puree well.

Makes 2 cups

Note: Open all windows and doors when roasting chiles, the odor of roasting chiles will cause you to cough.

Award Winning Salsa

Eating 5 or more Servings of colorful fruits and vegetables a day is part of an important plan for healthier living. That's because deeply hued fruits and vegetables provide the wide range of vitamins, minerals, fiber, and phytochemicals your body needs to maintain good health and energy levels, protect against the effects of aging, and reduce the risk of cancer and heart disease.
For more information go to www.5aday.com

NUTRITIONAL GUIDE
PER SERVING

CALORIES	28.5
FAT (G)	.2
SATURATED	0
UNSATURATED	0
PROTEIN (G)	1
CARBOHYDRATES (G)	6.8
FIBER (G)	1.2
CHOLESTEROL (MG)	0
SODIUM (MG)	238

INGREDIENTS

1	each	red bell pepper, roasted, seeded, small dice
1	each	yellow bell pepper, roasted, seeded, small dice
1	each	green bell pepper, roasted, seeded, small dice
1	each	red onion, peeled, small dice
1	each	jalapeño, roasted, minced
1	each	fresno chile, roasted, minced
1	teaspoon	lime juice
1	each	green onion, sliced
2	tablespoons	cilantro leaves, coarse chop
1	each	heirloom tomato, small dice
2	teaspoons	salt
1	teaspoon	olive oil

METHOD

* Light the grill, allow the flame to burn down to a medium fire.
* Brush peppers, and green onion with oil.
* Grill until brown, but not burned, about 8 minutes. Turn frequently.
* Peel, seed, and de vain peppers/chiles.
* Prep all ingredients as outlined above, place in bowl.
* Add lime juice, cilantro and salt to taste.
* Chill for one hour.

Makes 3 ½ cups

Salsa Verde
(Green Salsa)

TOMATILLOS

Tomatillos look like small green tomatoes encased in a papery husk. They're pleasantly tart, and principally used to make Mexican salsas, particularly salsa verde. They're good raw, but many chefs cook them briefly in order to enhance their flavor.

NUTRITIONAL GUIDE
PER SERVING

CALORIES	32
FAT (G)	.8
SATURATED	0
UNSATURATED	0
PROTEIN (G)	1.2
CARBOHYDRATES (G)	6.4
FIBER (G)	1.8
CHOLESTEROL (MG)	0
SODIUM (MG)	270

INGREDIENTS

SERVINGS 10

1 ½	pounds	tomatillos
1	each	serrano pepper
1	clove	garlic, peeled
1	tablespoon	cilantro, coarse chop
4	ounces	white onion, small dice
1	teaspoon	salt

METHOD

* Peel and boil tomatillos for 15-20 minutes.
* Drain and reserve ½ cup liquid.
* Place tomatillos, serrano peppers and garlic into a blender. Slowly incorporate liquid as needed.
* Process until slightly chunky.
* Transfer into a bowl.
* Add cilantro, onions and salt.
* Mix well.

Makes 2 ½ cups.

Note: Although great chilled, I like to serve it immediately, while still warm.

Salsa de Frutas
(Fruit Salsa)

FRUIT

Fruits and vegetables provide the vitamins, minerals, and fiber the body needs.

Most fruits and vegetables are low in calories and fat and contain water and fiber which provide a feeling of fullness.

NUTRITIONAL GUIDE
PER SERVING

CALORIES	50
FAT (G)	.4
SATURATED	0
UNSATURATED	.1
PROTEIN (G)	1.1
CARBOHYDRATES (G)	12.6
FIBER (G)	2.6
CHOLESTEROL (MG)	0
SODIUM (MG)	92

INGREDIENTS

SERVINGS   12

4	ounces	pineapple, peeled, small dice
8	ounces	peaches, small dice
6	each	strawberries, slice 1/8 inch thick
½	each	jalapeños, finely chopped
2	tablespoons	cilantro, coarse chop
2	ounces	red onion, small diced
½	each	jalapeños, finely chopped
2	tops	green onions (green only)
½	teaspoons	salt
3	tablespoons	water
½	each	orange juice

METHOD

* In a large bowl, combine all ingredients.
* Chill and serve after 2 hours.

Note: This salsa is great as a dip or served with grilled, fish, chicken or pork.

See picture of salsa on page 90.

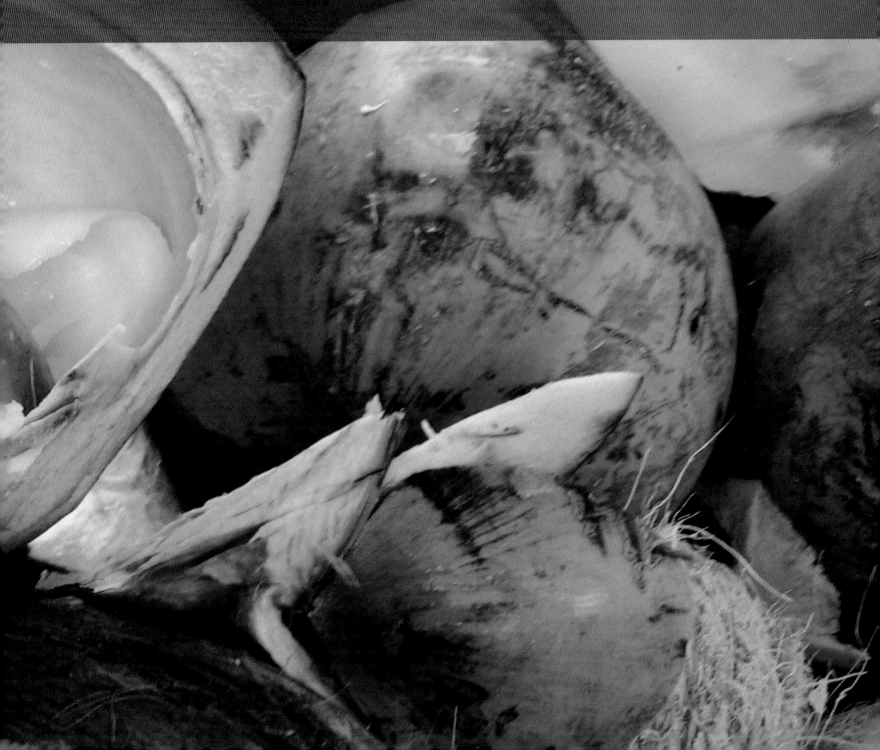

soup

Sopa de Conchitas
(Shell Soup)

POMEGRANATE

The name pomegranate comes from the Latin word for "fruit of many seeds". Because of its numerous seeds and its red color, the pomegranate has been linked with fertility since ancient times.

Also, the juice from pomegranates is one of nature's most powerful antioxidants.

NUTRITIONAL GUIDE
PER SERVING

CALORIES	389
FAT (G)	4.4
SATURATED	.9
UNSATURATED	3.5
PROTEIN (G)	17
CARBOHYDRATES (G)	70
FIBER (G)	3.2
CHOLESTEROL (MG)	9
SODIUM (MG)	673

INGREDIENTS

SERVINGS 6

2	teaspoons	extra virgin olive oil
2	ounces	brown onion, peeled and small dice
7	ounces	large pasta shells
2	cups	chicken stock
8	ounces	canned tomato puree
4	ounces	ham slices, lean, small dice
8	ounces	corn kernels, fresh or canned (drained and rinsed)

METHOD

* In a medium sauce pan, heat the oil.
* Add the shells, stirring constantly until golden brown.
* Add onions, cook until soft.
* Add chicken stock and tomato puree.
* Cover, simmer over low heat for 20 minutes until shells are tender.
* Add ham and corn, cook for 5-10 minutes.

Makes 4 cups

This is the soup my mom makes us when we are "sick". It is lite and filling and it always made me feel better.

Fideos
(Noodle Soup)

CACTUS PRICKLY PEAR

The flavor of a ripe prickly pear cactus fruit depends on the variety.

You can eat them raw, at room temperature or chilled, alone or with lemon juice. They can be cooked into jams and preserves or cooked down into a syrup as a base for jelly and candy. This syrup can be reduced even further into a dark red or black paste that is fermented into a potent alcoholic drink called "coloncha." The fruit pulp can be dried and ground into flour for baking into small sweet cakes, or stored for future use.

INGREDIENTS

3	ounces	Mexican fideos
½	teaspoon	olive or canola oil
1	ounce	onion, peeled and small dice
4	ounces	tomato puree
8	ounces	chicken stock

METHOD

* In a sauce pan, heat oil. Sauté fideos until golden brown.
* Add tomato puree and chicken stock.
* Simmer for 15-20 minutes over low heat, until noodles are tender.
* Serve in a medium bowl.

Makes 2 cups.

Note: Fideos can be found either in the pasta section of the grocery store or the Latin food section. Replacement options are angel hair pasta and vermicelli.

This is a good recipe to make from left over chicken soup (see page 94).
Utilize the stock amount listed above and add 6 ounces of chicken from the soup.

NUTRITIONAL GUIDE
PER SERVING

CALORIES	216
FAT (G)	1.8
SATURATED	.4
UNSATURATED	1.4
PROTEIN (G)	9.9
CARBOHYDRATES (G)	40
FIBER (G)	2.5
CHOLESTEROL (MG)	1
SODIUM (MG)	428

Gazpacho Andalucía
(Analucian Gazpacho)

TOMATOES

Biologically, they're a fruit. Nutritionally, they're a vegetable. A medium ripe tomato has a mere 25 calories, but provides a good dose of both vitamin A and vitamin C. Look for plump, heavy tomatoes with smooth skins that smell fragrant. The absence of an aroma indicates the tomato was likely picked while unripe and will likely never fully ripen.

NUTRITIONAL GUIDE
PER SERVING

CALORIES	130
FAT (G)	5.4
SATURATED	.8
UNSATURATED	4.6
PROTEIN (G)	3.3
CARBOHYDRATES (G)	192
FIBER (G)	2.9
CHOLESTEROL (MG)	0
SODIUM (MG)	470

INGREDIENTS

SERVINGS   3

3	ounces	tomato
5	ounces	cucumber, peeled
3	ounces	onion, peeled
1	clove	garlic, peeled
5	ounces	red bell pepper, seeded
8	ounces	tomato juice, chilled
2	slices	french bread, day old, crust removed
1	tablespoon	extra virgin olive oil
2	tablespoons	sherry vinegar
1/8	teaspoon	white pepper
1	medium	hard boiled egg, peeled and sliced

METHOD

* In a blender or food processor, add tomato, cucumber, onion, garlic, red bell pepper and tomato juice.
* Pulse for a thick & chunky consistence.
* Add french bread, olive oil, cherry vinegar, tomato juice, pulse to combine.
* Serve in small bowl.
* Garnish with egg.

Makes 3 cups.

Note: Gazpacho must be served really cold. Chill if needed. I also chill the bowl.

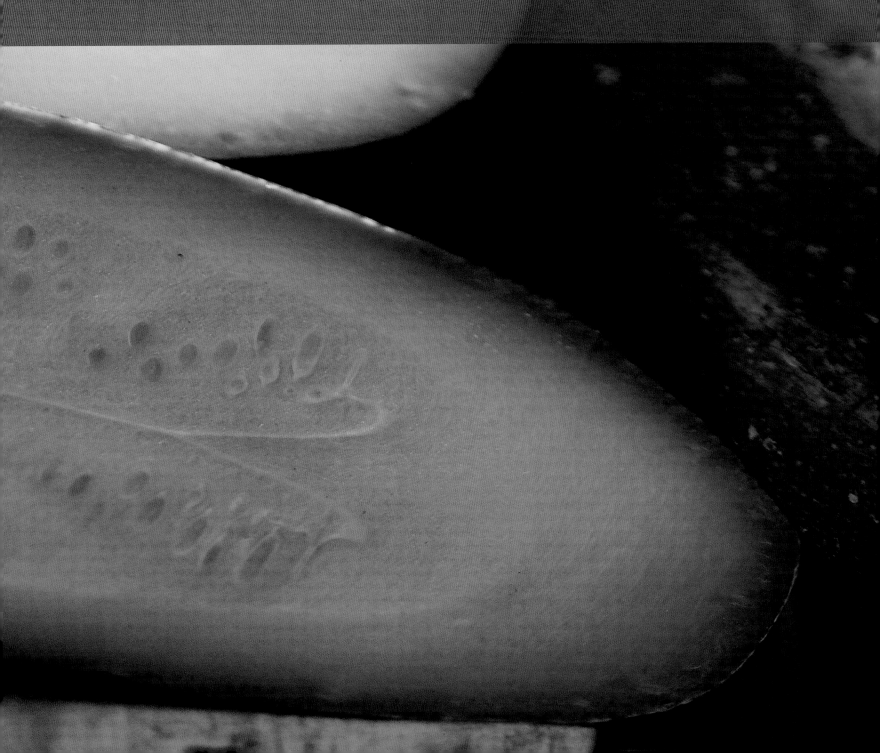

salads and vegetables

Ensalada de Mango Picante
(Spicy Mango Salad)

MANGOES

Fully loaded with nutrients, one average mango provides more than the daily requirement of vitamin C, two thirds of your needed Vitamin A, half of your Vitamin E, and one quarter of your fiber daily needs.

It is a great antioxidant and a useful contributor of potassium and iron.

NUTRITIONAL GUIDE
PER SERVING

CALORIES	460
FAT (G)	22.4
SATURATED	4.8
UNSATURATED	17.6
PROTEIN (G)	10.1
CARBOHYDRATES (G)	67.9
FIBER (G)	13.8
CHOLESTEROL (MG)	0
SODIUM (MG)	715

INGREDIENTS

1	clove	garlic, peel
7	each	basil leaves
1	ounce	extra virgin olive oil
2	ounces	Tabasco hot sauce
½	teaspoon	salt
8	ounces	lettuce leaves
2	ounces	red onion, peel, thin slice
6	ounces	hot house cucumber, thin slice
8	each	cherry tomatoes
1/8	each	hass avocado, ripe, firm, peeled and sliced
½	ounce	dried banana chips
1	teaspoon	pine nuts
1	tablespoon	dried cranberries
1	large	mango, ripe, firm

METHOD

* Wash and tear lettuce into bite size pieces. Soak in cold water.
* Dressing: In a blender or food processor, combine garlic, fresh basil, olive oil pepper sauce and salt.
* Blend until basil is speckled, not pureed.
* Pour into a medium bowl, set aside.
* Peel the mangoes with a potato peeler. Place the mango on a cutting board and cut downward vertically along each side, following the contour of the pit. You should have two large pieces of mango. Repeat with remaining mangoes.
* To make a fan: Place the mango pieces flat side down. Cut lengthwise, 8 slits, equal distance apart, leaving 1 inch uncut at one end. Carefully transfer the mango slices onto a platter.
* Drain the lettuce well.
* Arrange lettuce at the bottom of a flat plate.
* Layer tomatoes, onions, cucumber and avocado.
* Dip the mango slices in the basil dressing sauce. Place generously covered mango, flat side down, on top of greens. Gently push on the center of the mango to "fan out".
* Top your salad with banana chips, pine nuts and cranberries.

Curtido Centro Americano
(Central American Slaw)

INGREDIENTS

2	pounds	cabbage head, shredded
6	cups	water
1	teaspoon	salt
3	ounces	carrot, peeled and grated
4	ounces	brown onion, peeled and thinly sliced
½	cup	water
½	cup	vinegar
1	tablespoon	dried oregano
1	teaspoon	red pepper flakes (optional)

ONIONS

When purchasing onions, look for dry outer skins free of spots or blemished. The onion should be heavy for its size with no scent.

High heat makes onions bitter. When sautéing onions, always use low or medium heat.

METHOD

* In a medium stock pot, bring water and a teaspoon of salt to a boil (the salt will brighten the green in the cabbage).
  The following process is called blanching:
* Submerge cabbage in water, remove immediately and place in ice bath (in order to stop the cooking process).
* In a large bowl, combine cabbage, carrots, onion, water, vinegar, oregano, and red pepper flakes.
* Place in refrigerator covered. Best after 6 hours.

Makes 8-10 cups

Note: Central American food is not typically spicy. The addition of the red pepper flakes is optional, dependant on personal taste.

NUTRITIONAL GUIDE
PER SERVING

CALORIES	31.5
FAT (G)	.3
SATURATED	0
UNSATURATED	0
PROTEIN (G)	1.4
CARBOHYDRATES (G)	7.3
FIBER (G)	.6
CHOLESTEROL (MG)	0
SODIUM (MG)	77

Ensalada de Nopalitos
(Prickly Salad)

NOPALITOS

However, forbidding the spines, this cactus is definitely worth eating. The pads are "cladodes" or "nopales" when they're whole, and "nopalitos" when they're diced.

INGREDIENTS

1	cup	nopales, sliced – fresh or bottled
1	small	red onion, thin slice
3	tablespoons	apple cider vinegar
4	tablespoons	cilantro, fine chop
½	teaspoon	fresh oregano, minced
½	cup	cotija cheese, crumbled (about 12 ounces)
1	teaspoon	olive oil
4	medium	tomatoes, small dice
1	head	romaine lettuce
5	each	radish, thin sliced
1	large	hass avocado, ripe, firm, peeled and sliced

METHOD

* In a large bowl, combine the nopales, onion, vinegar, cilantro and oregano.
* Allow it marinade for 15 to 30 minutes.
* Combine cotija cheese, olive oil, and tomatoes to the mixture.
* On a large serving platter, arrange lettuce along the rim.
* Transfer the mixture to the center of the lettuce.
* Garnish with radish and avocado.

Makes 5 Cups.

NUTRITIONAL GUIDE
PER SERVING

CALORIES	123
FAT (G)	7.6
SATURATED	1.6
UNSATURATED	
PROTEIN (G)	4.4
CARBOHYDRATES (G)	12.6
FIBER (G)	5.8
CHOLESTEROL (MG)	4
SODIUM (MG)	145

Ensalada de Mango y Queso
(Cheese and Mango Salad)

LIMON (LIME)

All citrus fruits are rich in vitamin C as well as other micro-nutrients, certain phytochemicals and fiber.

Citrus fruits also protect against infection and cancer. They are an essential element in any healthy diet.

INGREDIENTS

2	ounces	queso fresco, medium dice
1	tablespoon	cilantro, shredded
1	tablespoon	lime juice
2	ounces	red onion, peeled, medium dice
1	teaspoon	extra virgin olive oil
3	ounces	tomato
3	ounces	hot house cucumber
4	ounces	mango, peeled, sliced

SERVINGS   2

METHOD

* In a large mixing bowl, combine all ingredients.
* Gently toss.
* Chill for one hour.
* Serve on a decorative plate.

NUTRITIONAL GUIDE
PER SERVING

CALORIES	122
FAT (G)	5
SATURATED	1.8
UNSATURATED	3.2
PROTEIN (G)	4.8
CARBOHYDRATES (G)	16.6
FIBER (G)	2.3
CHOLESTEROL (MG)	16..6
SODIUM (MG)	150

Pico de Gallo
(Jicama Salad)

PICO DE GALLO

Growing up, this is the kind of snack we ate at home. And to this day, when I am craving something late at night and want some empty, but flavorful calories, this is my first choice.

The last time I visited Mexico, I was brought a plate with jicama, cucumber and lime as a starter. So yummy!

NUTRITIONAL GUIDE
PER SERVING

CALORIES	90
FAT (G)	.3
SATURATED	0
UNSATURATED	0
PROTEIN (G)	2.1
CARBOHYDRATES (G)	27
FIBER (G)	7.6
CHOLESTEROL (MG)	0
SODIUM (MG)	138

INGREDIENTS

SERVINGS 1

6	ounces	orange, segmented
6	ounces	jicama, peeled, cut into 1 inch large dice
4	ounces	cucumber, cut into 2 inches long, and cut ¼ lengthwise
1	each	lime
1	dash	salt
1	dash	ground cayenne pepper

METHOD

* Strategically place orange, jicama and cucumbers on a plate.
* Garnish with a lime wedge.
* Sprinkle with cayenne pepper and salt.

or

* In a large mixing bowl, combine all ingredients.
* Gently toss.
* Chill covered.
* Serve on a decorative plate.

Calabasitas con Elote
(Mexican Squash with Corn)

MEXICAN SQUASH

Squash is native to the western hemisphere with origins in Latin America as far back as 5500 BC. This squash may be round to elongated, green with white striations on the skin with a zucchini-like, soft fleshy interior.

Select firm, plump, and unblemished squash

NUTRITIONAL GUIDE
PER SERVING

CALORIES	69
FAT (G)	2
SATURATED	1.1
UNSATURATED	.9
PROTEIN (G)	4.2
CARBOHYDRATES (G)	10.6
FIBER (G)	1.6
CHOLESTEROL (MG)	6
SODIUM (MG)	481

INGREDIENTS

6	ounces	tomato, seeded, medium dice
8	ounces	Mexican squash, large ½ inch slices
4	ounces	canned corn, drained
2	ounces	monterey jack cheese, sliced
1	teaspoon	lowfat butter (optional)

METHOD

Baking Method

* Place all ingredients in baking dish.
* Top with cheese.
* Place in preheated oven and bake for 15 minutes at 375°.

Stove top method

* Place all ingredients in a sauté pan.
* Cook over medium to high heat for 5 minutes.
* Stir occasionally.
* Vegetables should be firm, not mushy.
* Top with cheese and:

    * cover, cook to melt cheese, approx. 3 minutes, or
    * place in broiler to brown cheese

Elote Asado
(Roasted Corn)

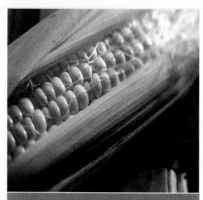

CORN

Corn is a versatile vegetable that is especially popular in Latin American cuisine. In addition to the kernels, the husks can be used for tamales. Good quality white or yellow corn should have fresh green, tightly fitting husks, with golden brown silk, and tip ends that are free of decay. Ears should be evenly covered with plump, consistently sized kernels. Avoid corn that has been on display with husks pulled back, or with discolored or dry-looking husks, stem ends, or kernels.

NUTRITIONAL GUIDE
PER SERVING

CALORIES	131
FAT (G)	.7
SATURATED	.1
UNSATURATED	0.5
PROTEIN (G)	5
CARBOHYDRATES (G)	32
FIBER (G)	3.9
CHOLESTEROL (MG)	0
SODIUM (MG)	8

INGREDIENTS

SERVINGS 1

On the streets of Mexico and Central America, the aroma of corn roasting is unmistakable...simply delicious. Enjoy this snack at home. Be creative and add your favorite healthy toppings.

cotija cheese
fat free margarine
lime
chile
cayenne
garlic
herbs

METHOD

* Heat the grill to a medium heat (you should be able to hold your hand about 4 inches above the grate for six to eight seconds). If using charcoal it should be glowing orange with a light layer of ash.
* Remove outer husk. Turn back inner husks; remove silks.
* Place on corn grill.
* Turn often.
* Roast 10 minutes.

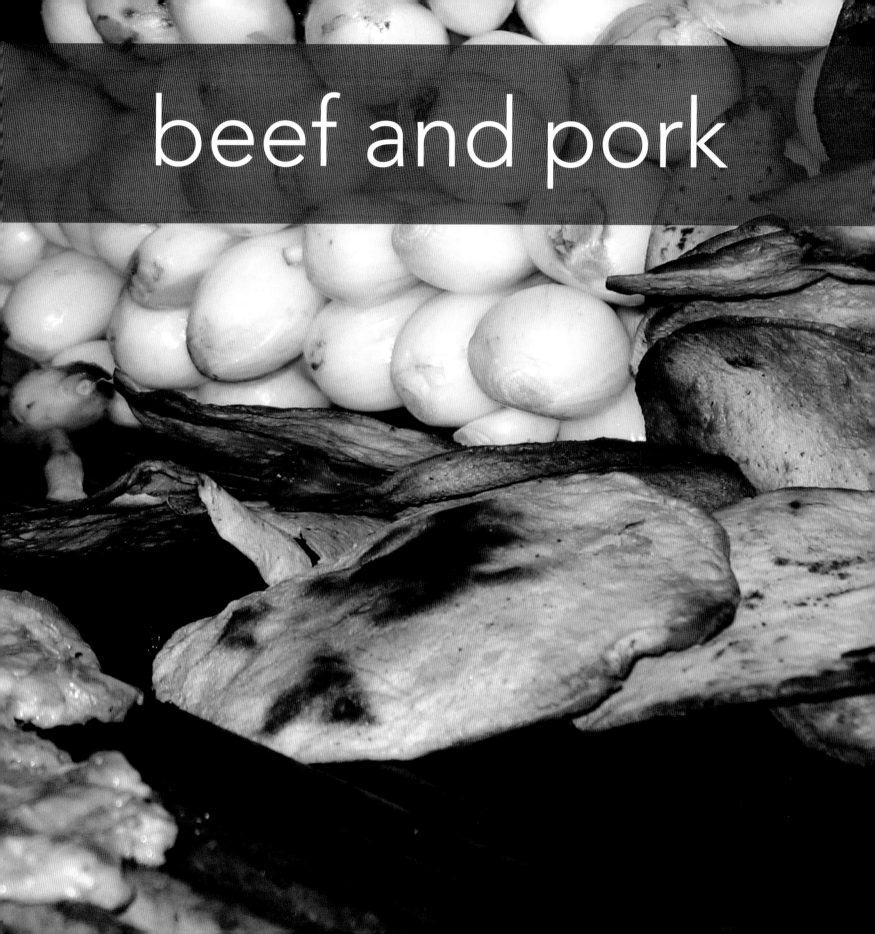

beef and pork

Caldo de Res
(Beef Soup)

ZUCCHINI

This food is very low in Saturated Fat and Cholesterol. It is also a good source of Thiamin, Riboflavin, Niacin and Iron, and a very good source of Dietary Fiber, Vitamin A, Vitamin C, Vitamin K, Vitamin B6, Folate, Magnesium, Phosphorus, Potassium, Copper and Manganese.

NUTRITIONAL GUIDE
PER SERVINGS

CALORIES	224
FAT (G)	7
SATURATED	2
UNSATURATED	5
PROTEIN (G)	20
CARBOHYDRATES (G)	20
FIBER (G)	3
CHOLESTEROL (MG)	33
SODIUM (MG)	1091

INGREDIENTS

12	cups	water
2	pounds	beef shank – crosscut
2	cloves	garlic, peeled
1	stalk	celery, cut into ½ inch pieces
4	ounces	brown onion, peeled, large dice
12	ounces	russet potatoes, peeled, cut into 1 inch dice
12	ounces	chayote, cut into 8 wedges
1	each	corn, husked, cut into 1 inch pieces
1	pound	cabbage, cut into 6 wedges
8	ounces	carrots, peeled, cut into 1 inch pieces
12	ounces	zucchini (italian style), cut into 1 inch pieces
¼	bunch	cilantro, rough chop
1	tablespoon	salt

METHOD

* Chop the beef shank into large chunks, keeping some attached to the bone - the bone marrow is an important element of the recipe.
* In a large stock pot add meat, water, garlic, celery and onions.
* Bring to a boil, reduce the heat to medium.
* Cover and simmer for 2 hours.
* Skim off any foam and fat.
* Add potatoes, chayote, and corn. Simmer for 15-20 minutes.
* Add cabbage, carrots, zucchini, cilantro and salt. Cover, cook for 15 minutes.
* Adjust salt.
* Serve in large bowl. Garnish with lemon wedges.

Note: This soup is traditionally served with Spanish Rice (see page 124) and accompanied by chopped sides of onion and cilantro.

Also, in some parts of Mexico, Caldo de Res is garnished with banana slices.

Albondigas
(Meatball Soup)

GROUND BEEF

New data from the U.S. Department of Agriculture show that a 3-ounce cooked serving of 95 percent lean ground beef, has five grams of total fat, which meets the government guidelines for lean, while providing an abundance of essential nutrients - Protein, Zinc, vitamin B-12 and other nutrients, and a good source of Iron, Niacin, vitamin B-6 and Riboflavin.

It's even better to know that ground beef can provide these nutrients in a lean way.

NUTRITIONAL GUIDE	
PER SERVING	
CALORIES	259
FAT (G)	10
SATURATED	4.2
UNSATURATED	6.6
PROTEIN (G)	15.3
CARBOHYDRATES (G)	23
FIBER (G)	1
CHOLESTEROL (MG)	102
SODIUM (MG)	198

INGREDIENTS

SERVINGS 7

10	cups	chicken broth
1	pound	lean ground beef
2	large	eggs
4	ounces	long grain rice
3	ounces	carrots, peeled, grated
3	ounces	white onion, peeled, large dice
8	ounces	tomato sauce
6	ounces	potatoes, peeled, large dice
½	teaspoon	chicken bouillon
1	dash	salt and pepper
¼	teaspoon	dried oregano

METHOD

* In a large stock pot, heat the chicken broth over a medium heat.
* In a large bowl, combine ground meat, eggs, rice and carrots.
* Mix well and shape into 1-inch meatballs.
  (This recipe makes 14 golf ball size meatballs).
* When the broth simmers, add meatballs and onion.
* Cover and cook for 45 minutes.
* Add tomato sauce, potatoes, chicken bouillon, pepper and dried oregano.
* Cook for 20 minutes.
* Adjust the salt.
* Serve in large soup bowl.

Makes 7 cups

Note: My mom also adds zucchini and carrots and cooks for an additional 7-10 minutes right before serving.

Enchiladas Raquel
(Rachel's Enchiladas)

TORTILLAS

As the "bread" of Mexico, the tortila is much more nutritious than the corn itself because of the process of making corn into masa (classic corn dough).

This process, called nixtamalization, increases the protein value of corn by releasing bound niacin.

NUTRITIONAL GUIDE
PER SERVING

CALORIES	180
FAT (G)	7.9
SATURATED	2.9
UNSATURATED	5
PROTEIN (G)	8.5
CARBOHYDRATES (G)	19
FIBER (G)	2.2
CHOLESTEROL (MG)	30
SODIUM (MG)	279

INGREDIENTS

1	pound	extra lean ground beef
12	ounces	potato, peeled and quartered
3	ounces	water
6	ounce	tomatoes, canned
1	teaspoon	salt
2	cloves	garlic, peeled
4	ounces	onion, peeled and quartered
2	each	serrano chilies
4	cups	beef or vegetable stock
1	each	tostada (fried tortilla)
¼	teaspoon	pepper
1	dash	cumin
14	each	corn tortillas
12	ounces	monterey jack cheese

METHOD

* Place meat, potatoes, ground beef and water in pot.
* Cover, cook over low medium heat for 20 minutes, until potatoes are tender.
* Drain the juice and reserve.
* Mash the meat and potatoes together with a potato masher.
* Mix in ½ teaspoon of salt.
* In a blender, add reserved juice, canned tomatoes, ½ teaspoon of salt, garlic cloves, onions, serrano chiles, stock, tostada (to thicken sauce), pepper and cumin.
* Puree and transfer sauce into a saucepan.
* Simmer on low for 20 minutes.
* Dip tortilla into saucepan, carefully and quickly transfer onto a baking pan.
* Spoon 2 ounces of meat/potato filling onto the tortilla in an elongated manner.
* Roll the tortilla with the seam ending up at the bottom.
* Arrange rolls closely to one another.
* Repeat with each tortilla. Cover with more sauce.
* Place in an oven for 5~7 minutes at 375˚.
* Serve immediately.
* Sprinkle with crumbled cotija or queso fresco.

Makes 14 enchiladas.   Sauce makes 4 ½ cups

Carne Asada
(Charbroiled Skirt Steak)

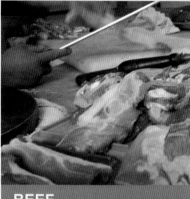

BEEF
Beef's fatty acid profile is generally misunderstood. Nearly half the fat in beef is monounsaturated, the same heart healthy fat found in olive oil that is championed by health professionals for its cholesterol lowering ability.

To find the leanest cuts of beef, look for the word "round" or "loin" in the name of the cut.

INGREDIENTS

3	pounds	skirt steak, fat trimmed, butterfly
1	cup	water
3	tablespoons	soy sauce, low sodium
4	ounces	brown onion, peeled, sliced
4	tablespoons	cilantro, tear into pieces
1	teaspoon	garlic cloves, peeled, sliced
1	teaspoon	extra virgin olive oil
1	teaspoon	unsalted meat tenderizer
¼	teaspoon	pepper
½	each	orange

METHOD

* In a large bowl, combine water, soy sauce, brown onion, cilantro, garlic, olive oil, meat tenderizer, pepper and orange.
* Add meat and marinade to fully cover both sides.
* Cover and refrigerate for at least four hours.
* Heat the grill to a medium heat (you should be able to hold your hand about 4 inches above the grate for six to eight seconds). If using charcoal it should be glowing orange with a light layer of ash.
* Place meat on grill.
* Turn steak once during cooking.
* Cook to desired doneness (5 minutes on each side for medium-rare).
* Serve with beans and salad.

NUTRITIONAL GUIDE
PER SERVING

CALORIES	212
FAT (G)	12.3
SATURATED	5.1
UNSATURATED	7.2
PROTEIN (G)	22.4
CARBOHYDRATES (G)	1
FIBER (G)	40
CHOLESTEROL (MG)	58
SODIUM (MG)	237

Chuletas con Fruta
(Pork Chops n' Fruit Salsa)

PORK

Today's lean pork means pork plays a vital part in a healthy diet.
Since the 1980s, the fat content of pork has been dramatically reduced. For example, the most popular selection of pork, the tenderloin, is now 42% lower in fat. This was achieved through: improved breeding and feeding practices and better trimming of fat, both at the processors and in the stores.

INGREDIENTS

1	pound	thick cut pork chop, fat trimmed
¼	teaspoon	salt
¼	teaspoon	pepper
1	dash	garlic powder
½	teaspoon	olive oil
6	ounces	Coca-Cola brand soft drink
½	teaspoon	canola oil

METHOD

* In a large bowl, combine salt, pepper, garlic powder, olive oil and coca cola.
* Mix well. Place pork chop in mixture.
* Cover and refrigerate for 45 minutes - allowing to marinade.
* In a large skillet, add canola oil.
* Sear both sides for 5 minutes each, until golden brown.
* Finish off in oven for 15-20 minutes at 325°.

Serve with fruit salsa (see page 52).

Makes 4-5 ounces cooked/per serving.

NUTRITIONAL GUIDE
PER SERVING

CALORIES	218
FAT (G)	12.8
SATURATED	4.4
UNSATURATED	8.4
PROTEIN (G)	24
CARBOHYDRATES (G)	0
FIBER (G)	0
CHOLESTEROL (MG)	68
SODIUM (MG)	51

poultry

Caldo de Pollo
(Chicken Soup)

INGREDIENTS

2	pounds	chicken breast, bone in, skinless
7	cups	water
3	ounces	brown onion, peeled, medium dice
2	teaspoons	chicken bouillon
2	stalks	celery, large dice
½	teaspoon	fresh oregano
3	each	carrot, peeled, large dice
8	ounces	potato, peeled, large dice

CHICKEN

Skinless chicken is one of the lowest-fat meats around. Although breast meat definitely has the lowest fat content, even skinless dark meat is comparatively low in fat and high in iron and other essential vitamins and minerals.

METHOD

* In a stock pot, add chicken, water, onion, chicken bouillon, celery and oregano.
* Cover, cook over medium heat for one hour.
* Remove chicken from stock pot, allow to cool for 5 minutes.
* Remove chicken meat from bones tearing into ¼ inch strips.
* Add chicken pieces back into stock pot.
* Add potatoes and carrots, cook for 15 minutes.
* Serve in a large soup bowl.

Makes 14 cups

Note: This soup also tastes great the next day, when reheated.

NUTRITIONAL GUIDE
PER SERVING

CALORIES	181
FAT (G)	1.6
SATURATED	.4
UNSATURATED	1.2
PROTEIN (G)	29.2
CARBOHYDRATES (G)	11
FIBER (G)	1.9
CHOLESTEROL (MG)	70
SODIUM (MG)	154

Citrus Chipotle Skewers

CHIPOTLE CHILES

Chipotle Chile is the dried, smoked, and ground fruit known as jalapeño of Capsicum annum. The product is made from chile peppers grown in northern and southern Mexico. Chipotle has a distinctive, smoky, sweet, meaty flavor with a moderately high heat level.

NUTRITIONAL GUIDE
PER SERVING

CALORIES	209
FAT (G)	1.6
SATURATED	.4
UNSATURATED	1.2
PROTEIN (G)	27.6
CARBOHYDRATES (G)	20.6
FIBER (G)	1.1
CHOLESTEROL (MG)	65
SODIUM (MG)	182

INGREDIENTS

SERVINGS 8

3	pounds	chicken breast, boneless, skinless
7	ounces	chipotle peppers in adobe sauce
12	ounces	frozen orange juice
4	ounces	tangerine juice
3	ounces	brown onion, peeled and sliced
4	cloves	garlic, minced
¼	teaspoon	pepper
4	tablespoons	olive oil
1	tablespoon	salt
2	medium	oranges for garnish
48		metal or bamboo skewers

METHOD

* Cut chicken breast into strips on a diagonal into ½ – 1 inch slices. Each skewer should weigh approximately 1.5 ounces. Thread chicken onto skewers. Place skewers into bowl.
* Remove chipotle peppers from sauce, chop coarse.
* In a large bowl combine orange juice, tangerine juice, onions, garlic, pepper, olive oil and chopped chipotle peppers and remaining adobe sauce (reserving some sauce for garnish).
* Pour mixture over skewers, marinade refrigerated for 2-4 hours. Add salt to marinade just prior to cooking.
* Grill skewers over medium heat for 3 minutes on each side or until to desired doneness.
* Garnish with sectioned tangerines and drizzle reserved adobe sauce.

Makes 48 skewers

Note: The acidity in the orange tenderizes the chicken. Marinating longer (overnight) can produce a better result.

Skewers are excellent as an appetizer as well as an entree. This recipe is also great with whole chicken breast. Make sure chicken cooks fully, until juices run clear, or it reaches an internal temperature of 160°.

Fajitas de Pollo
(Chicken Fajitas)

PEPPERS

Although most chili peppers are indigenous to South America, they are used and grown around the world. Hot peppers are used in abundance in Mexican, South American, Indonesian, African and Oriental cooking, while the milder peppers are common in European and North American recipes. And, peppers have been cultivated for thousands of years for their medicinal properties, known for lowering blood pressure and cholesterol, in addition to their culinary purposes.

NUTRITIONAL GUIDE
PER SERVING

CALORIES	117
FAT (G)	2.5
SATURATED	.3
UNSATURATED	2.2
PROTEIN (G)	15
CARBOHYDRATES (G)	9.3
FIBER (G)	1.8
CHOLESTEROL (MG)	35
SODIUM (MG)	323

INGREDIENTS

SERVINGS 6

1	pound	chicken breast halves, boneless, skinless
½	teaspoon	olive oil
2	teaspoon	lite soy sauce
1	medium	orange, juiced
1	medium	lime, juiced
1	tablespoon	cilantro, fine chop
2	cloves	garlic, minced
1	teaspoon	seasoned salt
1	teaspoon	pepper
1 ½	teaspoons	canola oil
3	ounces	red bell pepper, seeded, sliced lengthwise
3	ounces	green bell pepper, seeded, sliced lengthwise
5	ounces	red onion, peeled, thin slice
1	each	jalapeño, seeded, small dice
1	tablespoon	soy sauce, low sodium

METHOD

* Slice chicken breasts into ½ inch slices.
* In medium bowl, combine olive oil, lite soy sauce, orange juice, lime juice, cilantro, garlic, seasoned salt, pepper.
* Pour mixture over chicken. Stir to fully coat.
* Cover, refrigerate and allow to marinade for 2-4 hours.
* Heat canola oil in a large skillet over a high heat - to achieve stir-fry.
* Drain excess marinade from chicken.
* Add chicken to skillet, saute for 3 minutes - until golden brown.
* Add red an green bell peppers, onion and jalapeños.
* Sprinkle soy sauce over vegetables, stir constantly .
* Vegetables should be cooked but still firm.
* Serve immediately.

Note: This recipe also works great with beef and shrimp.

Fricasse de Pollo
(Chicken Fricasée)

INGREDIENTS

1 ½	pounds	chicken, skinless
¼	cup	olive oil
1	each	onion, peeled, sliced
½	cup	white wine
3	tablespoons	flour
2	cups	chicken stock
2	medium	bay leaves
4	ounces	tomato puree
2	teaspoons	salt
1	teaspoon	pepper
6	ounces	potato, peeled, medium dice
½	cup	peas, frozen
¼	cup	olives

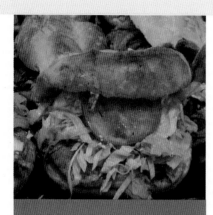

As a time consuming measure, I try to make several dishes out of one basic dish.

An example would be, one day I would eat the fricasse for dinner and pack myself lunch for the next day with the leftover chicken, bread, lettuce and tomato - A yummy torta *(Mexican sandwich)*.

METHOD

* Heat the olive oil in a large pan. Add chicken.
* Sear all sides.
* Add onion. Cook until soft.
* Add wine. Reduce (allow to absorb) for 10 minutes.
* Combine the flour with cold chicken stock.
* Add stock combination to the pan. Simmer.
* Add tomato puree, salt, pepper, and potatoes.
* Cover, simmer for 20 minutes.
* Add peas and olives.
* Cook for 10 minutes.

NUTRITIONAL GUIDE
PER SERVING

CALORIES	255
FAT (G)	11.3
SATURATED	1.8
UNSATURATED	9.5
PROTEIN (G)	24.6
CARBOHYDRATES (G)	12.7
FIBER (G)	1.6
CHOLESTEROL (MG)	53
SODIUM (MG)	918

Chile Relleno
(Stuffed Chile)

INGREDIENTS

3	large	pasilla chiles
1	teaspoon	extra virgin oil
1	ounce	brown onion, small dice
1	clove	garlic, minced
1	pound	ground chicken
2	each	scallion tops (green), sliced
½	teaspoon	seasoned salt
½	teaspoon	chili flakes

METHOD

CHILES: The chiles should be fresh, firm and shiny. Avoid using chiles that are dull, soft and wrinkled, they are old and will be too soft after they have been seared and skinned. The fresher they are, the easier they will skin and handle when stuffing and cooking. In order to skin the chiles they must be seared on the outside until black. Ideally you want them seared, but still firm.

* Place chiles over a high flame. This should be done quickly, be careful not to over cook the chilies.
* After roasting, place the chiles in a plastic bag for 10 minutes. The sweat effect allows for easier skin removal.
* After peeling the chile, make a slit on one side about ¾ of the length of the chiles and remove the seeds and veins being careful not to rip the chile. The seeds and veins are what gives the chiles most of their "heat", so the more you remove, the more mild they will be.
* Place the chiles on paper towels and gently wipe them dry.
* In a skillet, heat oil, add garlic and onions, cook for 3 minutes until translucent.
* Add ground chicken, scallions, seasoned salt and chili flakes,
* Cook until chicken is golden brown.
* Carefully spoon chicken into the roasted chiles.
* Serve on a pool of warm Salsa de mi Abuelita (see page 44)

Beverages
is another great way to incorporate fruits and vegetables into your healthy diet.

Did you know that a glass of orange juice counts as two servings of fruit?

NUTRITIONAL GUIDE
PER SERVING

CALORIES	235
FAT (G)	9.8
SATURATED	2.4
UNSATURATED	7.4
PROTEIN (G)	28
CARBOHYDRATES (G)	8.3
FIBER (G)	2.1
CHOLESTEROL (MG)	83
SODIUM (MG)	349

seafood

Siete Mares
(Seven Seas Soup)

SEAFOOD

Not only is seafood delicious, but it's nutritious as well. It's a delightful addition to any meal and is an excellent, low-calorie source of many essential nutrients. Seafood contains about twenty percent of the high quality proteins of red meat and poultry. It is also low in fat and most of the fat it has is poly-unsaturated.

NUTRITIONAL GUIDE
PER SERVING

CALORIES	460
FAT (G)	8.4
SATURATED	1.4
UNSATURATED	7.0
PROTEIN (G)	68.7
CARBOHYDRATES (G)	37
FIBER (G)	4.1
CHOLESTEROL (MG)	275
SODIUM (MG)	1600

INGREDIENTS

SERVINGS 3

6	ounces	red potato, medium dice
6	cups	water
3	ounces	celery, large dice
4	ounces	onion, peeled, medium dice
1	clove	garlic
1	whole	jalapeño
8	ounces	tomato sauce
2	large	scallops
3	ounces	clams
4	ounces	cooked crab legs
6	ounces	halibut, large pieces
4	ounces	shrimp, medium-large, unpeeled
4	ounces	squid, cleaned, sliced
4	ounces	octopus
1	tablespoon	cilantro, coarsely chopped
4	ounces	tomato, diced
1	teaspoon	salt
2	tablespoons	lime, juiced

METHOD

* In a large stock pot, add water, red potatoes, celery, onion, garlic and jalapeño.
* Simmer for 15 minutes, until potatoes are tender.
* Add tomato sauce, scallops, clams, crab legs, halibut, shrimp, squid, octopus, cilantro, tomato and salt.
* Simmer for 5 minutes.
* Add lime juice.
* Serve in a large bowl.

Coctel de Camarón
(Shrimp Cocktail)

SHRIMP

Shrimp are anything but small in their nutrient density. A food ranking system qualified shrimp as an excellent source of vitamin B12, vitamin D, selenium, and unusually low-fat, low-calorie protein. Pictured above is another way to prepare a cocktail, cooked shrimp with sauce on the side, and lime.

INGREDIENTS

¼	pound	shrimp, 21-25 count
1 ½	cups	water
1	clove	garlic
2	each	peppercorns
1	small	bay leaf
2	ounces	cucumber, peeled, small dice
2	ounces	roma tomato, small dice
2	ounces	brown onion, peeled, small dice
1	teaspoon	cilantro, chopped
3	ounces	hass avocado, ripe, firm, medium dice
1	tablespoon	lime juice
1	tablespoon	ketchup
1	tablespoon	bottled hot sauce
1	dash	salt

METHOD

* In a large stock pot, add water, garlic, peppercorn and bay leaf.
* Bring water to a boil. Lower heat.
* Add shrimp, cook for 3 minutes.
* Drain shrimp. Reserve liquid.
* Remove bay leaf.
* Allow liquid and shrimp to cool. Refrigerate to chill.
* In al large bowl, combine cucumber, tomato, onion, cilantro, avocado, lime juice, ketchup and hot sauce.
* Add cooled shrimp liquid and shrimp.
* Adjust salt .
* Serve in a glass container.

Makes 2 - 16 ounce cocktails.

Note: Do not over cook - shrimp will become tough.
      Shrimp are done as soon as they become orange/pink.

NUTRITIONAL GUIDE
PER SERVING

CALORIES	121
FAT (G)	5
SATURATED	0.8
UNSATURATED	2.6
PROTEIN (G)	12.7
CARBOHYDRATES (G)	7.3
FIBER (G)	2.3
CHOLESTEROL (MG)	86
SODIUM (MG)	332

Huachinango a la Veracruzano
(Veracruz Style Snapper)

FISH

Because many diets now specify poly-unsaturated fat, rather than saturated fat, fish and shellfish make excellent main dishes. Some fish are relatively high in fat such as salmon, mackerel and catfish. However, the fat is primarily unsaturated.

INGREDIENTS

SERVINGS   2

8	ounces	red snapper fillets
2	large	banana leaves
4	each	green olives
4	ounces	tomato, slliced
½	each	whole pimientos, sliced
2	ounces	white onion, peeled and sliced
½	teaspoon	extra virgin olive oil
1	medium	jalapeño
1	teaspoon	dry oregano
1	tablespoon	lime juice
½	teaspoon	garlic salt

METHOD

* Clean the fish removing any bones.
* Line a baking pan with banana leaves.
* Place fish on banana leaves.
* Arrange tomatoes, pimentos and olives over fish.
* In medium bowl, combine, onions, olive oil, jalapeño, dry oregano, lime juice and garlic salt.
* Pour mixture over fish.
* Fold over the banana leaves making, fully enclosing the fish.
* Place in a preheated oven and cook for 15-20 at 375˚.

Note: Parchment paper may be used if banana leaves are not available.

Traditionally this recipe is made with a whole red snapper. I opted for an easier and more accessible (than obtaining a whole fish) version.

NUTRITIONAL GUIDE
PER SERVING

CALORIES	231
FAT (G)	10
SATURATED	1.5
UNSATURATED	8.5
PROTEIN (G)	24.9
CARBOHYDRATES (G)	12.5
FIBER (G)	1.7
CHOLESTEROL (MG)	42
SODIUM (MG)	795

Paella
(Typical Spanish Rice Dish)

SHELLFISH

Eating shellfish are beneficial to your health since they are very rich in vitamins and minerals, while still very low in fat. Fish and shellfish also contain Omega 3 Polyunsaturated acids, which cannot be produced by the body.

NUTRITIONAL GUIDE
PER SERVING

CALORIES	560
FAT (G)	10.6
SATURATED	1.8
UNSATURATED	8.8
PROTEIN (G)	31
CARBOHYDRATES (G)	58.6
FIBER (G)	3
CHOLESTEROL (MG)	71
SODIUM (MG)	1156

INGREDIENTS

SERVINGS 3

1	tablespoon	extra virgin olive oil
1	clove	garlic, minced
6	ounces	assorted colors bell peppers, seeded and medium dice
4	ounces	red onion, peeled and medium dice
¼	teaspoon	saffron threads
2	ounces	white wine
1	teaspoon	parsley, minced
6	ounces	chicken breast halves, skinless, sliced into ½ inch strips
1	cup	jazmin rice
2 ¼	cups	chicken stock
1	teaspoon	salt
1	dash	pepper
4	each	shrimp
4	each	clams
4	each	mussels
1	tablespoon	green peas, cooked

METHOD

* Heat the paella pan or skillet, add olive oil.
* Sauté the peppers, garlic, saffron and onions, 2-3 minutes, until soft.
* Add wine, reduce (allow to absorb) ½ by cooking.
* Add chicken sauté for 3-5 minutes.
* Add rice, sauté for 5 minutes until rice is clear.
* Add stock, salt and pepper.
* Cover, cook for 7 minutes.
* Add shrimp, clams and mussels.
* Cover and cook for an additional 10 minutes or until all the liquid is absorbed.
* Garnish with peas.

Makes 6 cups

Note: The quality of the saffron is key to the overall flavor.

beans, rice & nuts

Frijoles Charros
(Cowboy Beans)

BEANS

Dried beans are rich in protein, calcium, phosphorus and iron. Their high protein content, along with the fact that they're easily grown and stored, make them a staple throughout many parts of the world where animal protein is scarce or expensive

INGREDIENTS

5	cups	water
8	ounces	pinto beans
5	slices	bacon, cut into 1 inch pieces
1	clove	garlic, peeled
1	each	jalapeño
4	ounces	brown onion, peeled, large dice
1	tablespoon	salt
1	teaspoon	pepper

METHOD

* Rinse beans. Place in a large stock pot, cover with water and soak overnight.
* Cook beans for 2 hours, covered over medium heat. Add water if needed.
* In a medium skillet, render bacon.
* Add bacon, garlic, jalapeño, onion, salt and pepper. Cook for one hour.
* Serve with avocado, cotija cheese, and warm tortillas.

NUTRITIONAL GUIDE
PER SERVING

CALORIES	57
FAT (G)	.8
SATURATED	.3
UNSATURATED	.5
PROTEIN (G)	3.7
CARBOHYDRATES (G)	9.2
FIBER (G)	3.6
CHOLESTEROL (MG)	1
SODIUM (MG)	440

Casamiento
(Marriage: Red Beans and Rice)

SOFRITO

Sofrito is the base for some Puerto Rican and Caribbean dishes.

Containing blended peppers, tomato, onion, recao, garlic and onion, it can be made from scratch or purchased pre-made (see Casamiento recipe).

Sofrito can be added to beans, rice, soups and stews.

INGREDIENTS

8	ounces	dry red beans
3	ounces	water
4	ounces	brown onion, peeled, large piece
1 ½	teaspoons	salt
2	tablespoons	olive oil
4	ounces	brown onion, peeled, small dice
1	clove	garlic, peeled, finely sliced
3	cups	long grain white rice, cooked (follow instructions on package)
3	tablespoons	Goya brand sofrito

METHOD

* Sort and wash beans under cold running water.
* Soak 8 ounces of beans with 3 cups of water overnight in a large pot.
* To cook: add onion (the large piece to be removed later), cover and simmer for 2 hours until beans are tender. Add water if need.
* Add salt. Simmer an additional 10 minutes.
* Remove onion.
* In a sauté pan, over medium-high flame, heat olive oil.
* Add onions and garlic until golden brown.
* Add beans with a slotted spoon, minimizing the amount of liquid.
* Add cooked rice, and sofrito, stir well.
* Cook for 7-10 minutes until all liquid is absorbed.

Makes 6 cups

NUTRITIONAL GUIDE
PER SERVING

CALORIES	243
FAT (G)	1.5
SATURATED	.03
UNSATURATED	1.97
PROTEIN (G)	7.9
CARBOHYDRATES (G)	48.8
FIBER (G)	5.4
CHOLESTEROL (MG)	0
SODIUM (MG)	57

Lentejas
(Lentils)

INGREDIENTS

8	ounces	lentils
5	cups	water
3	ounces	onion, peeled, small dice
3	ounces	carrot, peeled, small dice
3	ounces	celery, small dice
2	cloves	garlic, peeled, minced
3	ounces	leek, small dice
1	tablespoon	cilantro, chopped
1	teaspoon	salt

METHOD

* Place lentils, water, onion, carrots celery, garlic, leeks, cilantro and salt in a small pot.

* Cook, covered over medium heat for 45 minutes.

* Serve as a soup, entree or side dish.

Makes 5 cups.

LENTILS

Compared to other types of dried beans, lentils are relatively quick and easy to prepare. They readily absorb a variety of wonderful flavors from other foods and seasonings.

Legumes are excellent sources of soluble fiber and protein, though they should be combined with whole grain cereals, nuts, or seeds to make a complete protein.

NUTRITIONAL GUIDE
PER SERVING

CALORIES	148
FAT (G)	.5
SATURATED	.1
UNSATURATED	.4
PROTEIN (G)	11.2
CARBOHYDRATES (G)	26.3
FIBER (G)	12.6
CHOLESTEROL (MG)	0
SODIUM (MG)	437

Arroz Confetti
(Confetti Rice)

RICE

American-grown rice is a clean product that does not need washing or rinsing before or after cooking. Most U.S. rice is enriched with iron, niacin, thiamin, and folic acid. Rinsing rice, or cooking rice in excess water and draining, results in loss of enrichment and other water-soluble vitamins and minerals.

INGREDIENTS

1	cup	long grain rice
2	tablespoons	butter
2	ounces	brown onion, small dice
1 ½	cups	chicken stock or water
1	cup	frozen mixed vegetables
1	teaspoon	salt

METHOD

* Rinse and drain rice.
* In a medium pan, over a low heat, melt butter and sauté onion until softened.
* Add rice to pan.
* Cook until golden, stirring constantly. Be careful not to brown.
* Cover and simmer 15 to 20 minutes until water is almost all absorbed.
* Add frozen vegetables.
* Continue to cook until all liquid is absorbed, about 5 minutes.

Makes 3 ½-4 cups

Note: In order to make Spanish Rice (aka Mexican Rice) using this same basic recipe, replace ¼ cup stock with ½ cup tomato sauce.

NUTRITIONAL GUIDE
PER SERVING

CALORIES	162
FAT (G)	4
SATURATED	2.5
UNSATURATED	1.5
PROTEIN (G)	3
CARBOHYDRATES (G)	28
FIBER (G)	1.8
CHOLESTEROL (MG)	10
SODIUM (MG)	409

Frijoles de Colores
(Colorful Bean Salad)

BEANS

Each half-cup serving of dry beans provides six to seven grams of protein, which meets at least 10% of the Recommended Dietary Allowance (RDA) for protein, yet costs about 20 cents per serving.

NUTRITIONAL GUIDE
PER SERVINGS

CALORIES	123
FAT (G)	1.6
SATURATED	.2
UNSATURATED	1.4
PROTEIN (G)	6.2
CARBOHYDRATES (G)	22.7
FIBER (G)	4.4
CHOLESTEROL (MG)	0
SODIUM (MG)	156

INGREDIENTS

SERVINGS 16

16	ounces	garbanzo beans, canned
16	ounces	kidney beans, canned
16	ounces	black beans, canned
16	ounces	corn, canned
2	tablespoon	apple cider vinegar
1	tablespoon	extra virgin olive oil
2	ounces	roasted red bell pepper, from a jar, diced
6	ounces	green bell pepper, seeded, small dice
2	tablespoons	cilantro, fine chop
1	tablespoon	Italian parsley, fine chop

METHOD

* Rinse and drain all canned items.
* In a large bowl, combine all ingredients.
* Chill before serving for 15-20 minutes.

Note: To save time, look for the red peppers already roasted and in a jar.

Sopa de Frijoles Negros
(Black Bean Soup)

INGREDIENTS

8	ounces	dry black beans
5	cups	water
2	cloves	garlic
8	ounces	white onion, peeled, medium dice
4	ounces	ham hocks, small pieces
1	teaspoon	cumin
1	tablespoon	salt
¼	teaspoon	pepper
4	ounces	cilantro, fine chop
4	ounces	white onion, peeled, fine chop

BLACK BEANS

They are commonly referred to as turtle beans, probably in reference to their shiny, dark, shell-like appearance. With a rich flavor that has been compared to mushrooms, black beans have a velvety texture while holding their shape well during cooking.

METHOD

* Rinse beans. Place in a large stock pot, cover with water and soak overnight.
* Cook beans for 2 hours, covered over medium heat. Add water if needed.
* Add ham hocks, cumin, salt and pepper. Cook for one hour.
* Garnish with chopped cilantro and onion.

Makes 4 cups.

NUTRITIONAL GUIDE
PER SERVING

CALORIES	127
FAT (G)	1.7
SATURATED	.5
UNSATURATED	1.2
PROTEIN (G)	8
CARBOHYDRATES (G)	21
FIBER (G)	5.4
CHOLESTEROL (MG)	6
SODIUM (MG)	931

desserts

Plátano Macho
(Honey Baked Plantain)

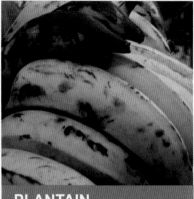

PLANTAIN

The plantain, a very large, firm variety, is also referred to as a "cooking banana" and is extremely popular in Latin American countries. It has a mild, almost squash like flavor and is used very much as a potato would be in the United States.

Plantains are high in carbohydrates and low in protein and fats; they're also rich in potassium and vitamin C.

NUTRITIONAL GUIDE
PER SERVING

CALORIES	141
FAT (G)	.3
SATURATED	0
UNSATURATED	0
PROTEIN (G)	1.2
CARBOHYDRATES (G)	37.3
FIBER (G)	2.1
CHOLESTEROL (MG)	0
SODIUM (MG)	4

INGREDIENTS

1	each	plantain, ripe
1	tablespoon	honey
1	large	banana leaf

SERVINGS 2

METHOD

* Place plantain in a baking dish.
* Make two small slices in the peel (air holes).
* Place in preheated oven for 15-20 at 375°.
* Serve hot.
* Garnish with banana leaves.

Note: A yummy additional ingredient is a tablespoon of rum splashed on the plantain, after cooking.

Manzanitas
(Baked Apples)

APPLES

Because there are so many different varieties of apple, each with slightly different qualities than the next, producers grow different types of apples for different purposes.

NUTRITIONAL GUIDE
PER SERVING

CALORIES	272
FAT (G)	.9
SATURATED	.2
UNSATURATED	.7
PROTEIN (G)	.6
CARBOHYDRATES (G)	72.6
FIBER (G)	7.19
CHOLESTEROL (MG)	0
SODIUM (MG)	2

INGREDIENTS

36	ounces	granny smith apples
5	ounces	honey
1	each	lemon, juiced
¼	teaspoon	ground cinnamon

SERVINGS   4

METHOD

* Wash apples. Peel and core apples. Slice apples thru ¼ inch thick to resemble orange sections.
* In a medium bowl, mix together the apples, honey, lemon juice and cinnamon.
* Divide mixture and spoon into four separate baking containers or one pie container.
* Arrange apple segments in a uniform and neat order.
* Bake in a preheated oven at 375° for 15 minutes until tender and golden brown on top.

Makes 2 ½ cups

Note: When using decorative backing dishes, this simple dish can have a dramatic presentation.

Arroz con Leche
(Rice Pudding)

CINNAMON

Cinnamon is also known by the names Cassia, Sweet Wood, and Gui Zhi. In ancient times, it was added to food to prevent spoiling.

A new study by The US Department of Agriculture's Human Nutrition Research Center found cinnamon significantly reduces blood sugar levels in diabetics.

INGREDIENTS

1	cup	calrose medium grain rice
3	cups	water
12	ounces	evaporated milk, non fat
3	tablespoons	condensed milk, low fat
2	ounces	raisins
1	teaspoon	ground cinnamon

METHOD

* In a medium saucepan, combine rice, and water.
* Cook over low heat, covered, for 13 minutes, until tender.
* Add evaporated milk and condensed milk and raisins. Stir well.
* Cook 8-10 minutes.
* Rice should be moist, liquid (milk) should not be completely dry.
* Serve in individual plates.
* Garnish by sprinkling with cinnamon.

Makes 4 Cups

NUTRITIONAL GUIDE
PER SERVING

CALORIES	83
FAT (G)	.03
SATURATED	.01
UNSATURATED	.02
PROTEIN (G)	2.9
CARBOHYDRATES (G)	17.4
FIBER (G)	.08
CHOLESTEROL (MG)	1
SODIUM (MG)	29

beverages

Agua de Tamarindo
(Tamarind Drink)

INGREDIENTS

25	each	tamarind pods
1	gallon	water
1 ½	cups	sugar

TAMARIND

Also known as Indian date, the tamarind is the fruit of a tall shade tree native to Asia and northern Africa and widely grown in India. They were brought to Mexico from India and have made their way down to Central America. The tropical tamarind tree bears fruit in pods like large, brown beans. This fruit is tart tasting and has fiborous flesh and a flat stone at the center.

METHOD

*   Peel tamarind.
*   In a large mixing bowl, pour one gallon of boiling water over the tamarind.
*   Add sugar or sweetner.
*   Allow to soak for 45 minutes, stirring often to dissolve the sugar and tamarind pulp.
*   Strain through a sieve into a pitcher of ice and water.
*   Chill.
*   Serve with ice.

NUTRITIONAL GUIDE
PER SERVING

CALORIES	80
FAT (G)	0
SATURATED	0
UNSATURATED	0
PROTEIN (G)	.1
CARBOHYDRATES (G)	20
FIBER (G)	.2
CHOLESTEROL (MG)	0
SODIUM (MG)	8

Casi Mojito
(Almost Mojito)

STRAWBERRIES

One cup of fresh strawberries contains only 43 calories and an impressive nutritional profile. Looking at the figures, one cannot help notice that this fruit is not lacking in valuable nutrients, but is endowed with a healthy content of every vitamin and mineral except Vitamin B12.

INGREDIENTS

32	ounces	sparkiling mineral water
4	large	limes
1	tablespoon	mint leaves
8	packets	splenda

METHOD

* Crush mint leaves and the juice of the limes in a tall glass.
* Cover with sparkling mineral water.
* Add Splenda, or sweetener of choice.
* Fill glass with ice.
* Garnish with lime and mint sprigs.

Note: To make a Cuban Mojito, just add rum.

NUTRITIONAL GUIDE
PER SERVING

CALORIES	66
FAT (G)	0
SATURATED	0
UNSATURATED	0
PROTEIN (G)	1.1
CARBOHYDRATES (G)	22.2
FIBER (G)	1
CHOLESTEROL (MG)	0
SODIUM (MG)	5

COOKING METHODS

Grilling A quick dry-heat method over charcoal, wood or gas flames.

Pan Broiling A quick dry-heat cooking method using a pan on a stove top. No oil is used and the pan is uncovered.

Pan Frying A quick dry-heat cooking method using a pan with a small amount of oil. No lid is used. Also called sautéing.

Poaching Poaching is to cook in a liquid that is not actually bubbling at 165 to 180 degrees. It is usually used to cook delicate foods such as fish and eggs.

Roasting Roasting is to cook foods by surrounding them in dry heat usually in an oven. It can also be accomplished by spit roasting over an open fire or on an outdoor grill.

Sautéing Sautéing is to cook quickly in a small amount of fat. The pan should be preheated. This will allow the food to be seared quickly. Small pieces of foods such as diced onions must be stirred or otherwise kept in motion during sautéing. Larger cuts of vegetables or slices of meat are usually only turned once.

Simmering Cooking in a liquid just below the boiling point. Bubbles usually rise and break just below or at the surface. The temperature of the liquid is 185 to 205 degrees.

Steaming Steaming is cooking foods by exposing them directly to steam. It can be accomplished in a number of ways; on a rack above boiling liquid, by wrapping foods tightly, or in a covered pan allowing the food item to cook in its own steam. Steaming is a preferred method of cooking for vegetables since it minimizes the loss of nutrients. The vegetables can be cooked rapidly without agitation.

Stewing A slow moist-heat cooking method using a pot with a tight-fitting lid and cooking until the food is tender.

Stir Frying A quick dry-heat cooking method using a lightly oiled pan. Use high heat while continuously tossing ingredients. Any cut can be used as long as it is cut into thin and uniform strips.

Amino Acids	Organic compounds containing an amino group and a carboxylic acid group; proteins are composed of various proportions of about 20 common amino acids.
Antibodies	An immunoglobulin, a specialized immune protein, produced because of the introduction of an antigen into the body, and which possesses the remarkable ability to combine with the very antigen that triggered its production. The production of antibodies is a major function of the immune system and is carried out by a type of white blood cell called a B cell.
Calories	The amount of energy required to raise the temperature of one kilogram of water one degree Celsius and equal to 1000 small calories -- used especially to indicate the value of foods in the production of heat and energy.
Carbohydrates	Mainly sugars and starches, together constituting one of the three principal types of nutrients used as energy sources (calories) by the body. Carbohydrates can also be defined chemically as neutral compounds of carbon, hydrogen and oxygen.
Cellulose	A straight-chain polysaccharide composed of hundreds of glucose units linked by beta bonds. It is indigestible by humans and is a component of dietary fiber.
Cholesterol	A white crystalline substance, found in animal tissues and various foods, that is normally synthesized by the liver and is important as a constituent of cell membranes and a precursor to steroid hormones. Its level in the bloodstream can influence the pathogenesis of certain conditions, such as the development of atherosclerotic plaque and coronary artery disease.
Chronic	Lasting for a long period of time or marked by frequent recurrence, as certain diseases.
Dehydration	Excessive loss of body water. Diseases of the gastrointestinal tract that cause vomiting or diarrhea may, for example, lead to dehydration. There are a number of other causes of dehydration including heat exposure, prolonged vigorous exercise (e.g., in a marathon), kidney disease, and medications (diuretics).
Digestion	The process of transforming the foods we eat into units for absorption.
Energy	Power or ability to be active: strength of body or mind to do things or to work.
Enzymatic	Any of numerous proteins or conjugated proteins produced by living organisms and functioning as biochemical catalysts.
Fat	Compounds formed from chemicals called fatty acids. These fats compose a greasy, solid material found in animal tissues and in some plants. Fats are the major component of flabby material of our bodies, commonly known as blubber.
Fiber	The parts of plants that cannot be digested, namely complex carbohydrate. Also known as bulk or roughage.
Fructose	A sugar that occurs naturally in fruits and honey. Fructose has 4 calories per gram.
Gram (measure):	A unit of measurement of weight and mass in the metric system. In weight, a gram is equal to a thousandth of a kilogram. In mass, a gram is equal to a thousandth of a liter (one cubic centimeter) of water at 4 degrees centigrade.

Glucose	The simple sugar (monosaccharide) that serves as the chief source of energy in the body. Glucose is the principal sugar the body makes. The body makes glucose from proteins, fats and, in largest part, carbohydrates. Glucose is carried to each cell through the bloodstream. Cells, however, cannot use glucose without the help of insulin. Glucose is also known as dextrose.
Glycogen	A polysaccharide, that is the main form of carbohydrate storage in animals and occurs primarily in the liver and muscle tissue. It is readily converted to glucose as needed by the body to satisfy its energy needs. Also called animal starch.
Hemoglobin	A protein that contains iron is the chief means of transporting oxygen in the body of vertebrate animals, occurs in the red blood cells, and is able to combine loosely with oxygen in regions.
Hormones	Chemical messengers that are secreted into the blood by one tissue and act on cells in another part of the body.
Hydrogenate	A chemical reaction in which hydrogen atoms are added to a fat.
Lipids	A group of fat-soluble compounds that includes triglycerides, sterols, and phospholipids.
Macro Nutrient	Nutrients, such as carbohydrate, fat, or protein, that are needed in relatively large amounts in the diet.
Metabolism	The chemical processes occurring within a living cell or organism that are necessary for the maintenance of life. In metabolism some substances are broken down to yield energy for vital processes while other substances, necessary for life, are synthesized.
Metabolize	To undergo change by metabolism.
Monounsaturated Fats	The carbon chain, contains one double bond.
Polyunsaturated Fats	The carbon chain, contains two or more double bonds.
Protein	Any of numerous nitrogen-containing substances that consist of chains of amino acids, are important parts of all living cells, are a necessary part of the human diet, and are supplied especially by such foods as meat, milk, and eggs.
Salt	A colorless or white crystalline solid, chiefly sodium chloride, used extensively in ground or granulated form as a food seasoning and preservative. Also called common salt, table salt.
Sugar	A sweet crystalline or powdered substance, white when pure, consisting of sucrose obtained mainly from sugar cane and sugar beets and used in many foods, drinks, and medicines to improve their taste. Also called table sugar.
Saturated Fat	A fatty acid completely filled by hydrogen, with all carbons in the chain linked by single bonds.
Starches	Naturally abundant nutrient carbohydrate, found chiefly in the seeds, fruits, tubers, roots, and stem pith of plants, notably in corn, potatoes, wheat, and rice, and varying widely in appearance according to source but commonly prepared as a white amorphous tasteless powder.
Unsaturated Fats	The carbon chain contains one or more double bonds.

SIZE MATTERS

A medium avocado in Florida, compared to an average medium avocado in California can vary by pounds. That is the very reason I have written the recipes in weights and measures, instead of listing items in units per ingredient.

At home, measuring your food for a day can help provide perspective on your portion sizes. When you monitor portion size, understand calorie content, and get regular physical activity, you can choose just about anything.

I have provided a chart outlining the weights and measures for fruits and vegetables as a tool for easy monitoring the portion size of the foods you enjoy.

	CALS	FAT
Alfalfa Sprouts, 1/2 cup, 1/2 oz.	5	0
Artichokes, Globe/French:		
1 medium, 4 1/2 oz.	65	0
Artichoke Heart, 1/2 cup, 3 oz.	40	0
Asparagus, raw/frozen		
4 medium spears, 2 oz.	15	0
Cuts & Tips, ½ cup, 3 oz.	25	<1
Bamboo Shoots, cooked, 1/4 c, 4 oz.	15	0
Beans: Green/Snap ½ cup, 2 oz.	20	0
Broadbeans, cooked, ½ cup, 3 oz.	90	0
Butterbeans, 1/2 cup, 3 oz.	90	0
Lima Beans, 1/2 cup, 3 oz.	90	0
Dry Beans, average all types:		
(Kidney, Brown, Haricot, Lima Mung, Navy, Pinto, Red, White)		
Raw, 2 Tbsp, 1 oz.	95	<1
1 cup, 7oz.	685	3
Alfalfa Sprouts, 1/2 cup, 1/2 oz	5	0
Artichokes, Globe/French:		
1 medium, 41/2 oz	65	0
Artichoke Heart, 1/2 cup, 3 oz.	40	0
Asparagus, raw/frozen		
4 medium spears, 2 oz.	15	0
Cuts & Tips, 1/2 cup, 3 oz.	25	<1
Bamboo Shoots, cooked, 1/4 c, 4oz	15	0
Beans: Green/Snap 1/2 cup, 2 oz.	20	0
Broadbeans/cooked, 1/2 cup, 3 oz.	90	0
Butterbeans, 1/2 cup, 3 oz.	90	0
Lima Beans, 1/2 cup, 3 oz.	90	0
Dry Beans, average all types:		
(Kidney, Brown, Haricot, Lima Mung, Navy, Pinto, Red, White)		
Raw, 2 Tbsp, 1 oz.	95	<1
1 cup, 7oz	685	3
Cooked, 1 oz.	35	0
1/2 cup, 3 oz	105	<1
Soybeans: Mature, dry, 1 oz.	110	5
Dry, 1/2 cup, 31/2 oz	385	18

	CALS	FAT
Cooked, 1/2 cup, 3 oz	105	5
Bean Sprouts, aver, 1/2 cup, 3 oz.	25	0
Beets, cooked: 1/2cup, slices, 3 oz.	25	0
1 beet, 2" diam, 2 oz.	17	0
Beet Greens, cooked, 1/2 cup, 2 1/2 oz.	20	0
Blacked Eyed Peas, cooked, 1/2 cup, 2 oz.	160	<1
Bok Choy (Chinese Chard) 3 oz.	12	0
Broccoli: Raw, 1/2 cup, 1 1/4 oz	12	0
1 spear (5 oz edible)	40	<1
Cooked, 1/2 cup, 3 oz.	25	0
Brussels Sprouts, cooked, 1/2c, 3 oz.	35	0
Cabbage, average all varieties:		
Raw, shred, 1/2 cup, 1 1/4 oz	8	0
Cooked, 1/2 cup, 2 1/2 oz	15	0
Carrots: cooked 1/2c slices, 2 1/4 oz	35	0
Raw, 1 medium, (7 1/2"), 3 oz.	33	0
Raw, 1 lb, (5-6 med)	175	<1
4 sticks (4"), 1 1/2 oz	15	0
Shredded, 1/2 cup, 2 oz.	25	0
Cauliflower, cooked:		
3 flowerettes, 1/2 cup, 1"pces, 3 oz.	15	0
1/2 medium (15oz raw)	100	0
Celeriac, 1/2 cup, raw, 2 3/4 oz	30	0
Celery, 1 stalk, 71/2", 1 1/2 oz	5	0
Diced, 1/2 cup, 2 1/4 oz	10	0
Chard (swiss), 1/2 cup, cooked, 3 oz.	20	0
Chick Peas (Garbanzo Beans):		
Dry, 1 cup, 6oz	550	10
Cooked, 1 cup, 6oz	270	4
Chicory/Witloof- See Endive		

	CALS	FAT
Greens, cooked, 1/2 cup, 2 1/2 oz	15	0
Water Chestnuts, 4 nuts	40	0
1/2 cup slices, 2 1/4 oz	65	0
Watercress, 10 sprigs, 1 oz	4	0
Yam, cooked, 1/2 cup, 2 1/2 oz	80	0
Mountain (Hawaii), cooked, 1/2 cup	60	0
Yardlong Bean, 1 pod, 1/2 oz	7	0
Zucchini, 1 medium, 10 oz	45	0
Acerola, 1 cup 20 pcs, 31/2 oz	30	0
Atemoya, 1/3 cup	95	<1
Apples, whole, average all varieties		
1 small (4 per lb), 4 oz	70	0
1 medium (3 per lb), 51/2 oz	90	0
1 large (2 per lb), 8 oz	135	<1
1 extra large, 11 oz.	170	1
Without skin, 1/2 medium	35	0
Apricots: 1 small (12 per lb)	17	0
1 medium (8 per lb), 2 oz	25	0
1 large (5-6 per lb) 3 oz	35	0
Avocado (wt. W/out seed):		
Average, 1/2 medium	160	15
California, 1/2 medium, 3 oz	150	15
Mashed/Puree, 1/2 cup, 4oz	200	20
Florida, 1/2 medium, 5 1/2oz	170	13
Mash/Puree, 1/2 cups, 4oz	125	10
1/2 cup cubed, oz	95	8
Banana: 1 small (4/lb). 4 oz	55	0
1 medium (3 per lb), 5 oz	80	<1
1 large (21/2 per lb), 7 oz	105	<1
W/out skin, 1 med, 3 1/4 oz	80	<1
1/2 cup, mashed, 4 oz	105	<1
Berries, average all types;		
(black/boysen/blueberries)		
1/2 cup, 21/2 oz	40	0
1 pint, 14 oz	220	1
Bread fruit, 1/2 cup, 4 oz	115	<1
Cantaloupe, 1/2 med (5' diam)	115	<1
1 slice, 2 1/2 oz (w/out skin)	20	0
1 cup pieces/balls, 5 1/2 oz	55	<1
Carambola (star fruit), 1 med	50	<1
Cassava, 1/3 cup	120	0
Cherimoya (Custard Apples)		
1/4 only, 5 oz	130	<1
Cherries: sweet, 8 fruit, 2 oz	40	1

	CALS	FAT
1/2 lb (30 cherries)	145	2
Sour, 6 fruit, 2 oz	25	0
1/2 lb (30 cherries)	100	<1
Coconut: Fresh, 1 piece, 1 oz	100	10
Shredded, fresh, 1/2 cup	140	14
Sweetened, dried, 1/2 cup	235	16
Cream, can, 1/2 cup	285	26
Milk, can, 1/2 cup	225	24
Water, 1/2 cup	20	<1
Crab Apples, 1/2 cup slices, 2 oz	40	0
Cranberries, 1/2 cup, 2 oz	20	0
Currants (per 1/2 cup):		
European Black, raw, 2 oz	35	0
Red & white, raw 2 oz	30	0
Dates -see dried fruits		
Durian, flesh, 4 oz	140	2
Elderberries, 1/2 cup, 2 1/2 oz	55	0
Feijoas, 1 median, 2 1/2 oz	35	0
Figs, green/black: 1 med, 2 oz	40	0
1 large, 3 oz	60	0
Fruit salad, fresh, average		
1/2 cup, 3 1/2 oz	60	0
1 cup, 7oz	120	0
Gooseberries raw, 1/2 cup, 2 1/2 oz	30	0
Grapefruit, average all types		
1/2 fruit, 8 1/2 oz (4 1/2 oz flesh)	40	0
1 Cup sections w /juice, 8 oz	75	0
Grapes: average, 1 cup, 5 1/2 oz	100	<1
1 small bunch, 4 oz	70	0
1 medium bunch, 7 oz	125	<1
1 large bunch, 1 lb	285	1
Granadilla, fresh, 3 1/2 oz	95	2
Ground cherries, 1/2 cup, 2 1/2 oz	35	0
Guava: 1 fruit, 4 oz	80	<1
1/2 cup, 3 oz	40	<1
Honey dew, 1 wedge (7'x2' wide)		
8 oz (with skin)	45	0
1 cup cubes/balls, 6 oz	60	0
Honey Murcots, 1 only, 5 oz	45	0
Jabotica, flesh, 4 oz	75	2
Jabotica, flesh, 1/8 aver, 4 oz	105	0
Jambos, flesh, oz	35	0
Java-plum, 4 plums, 1/2 oz	25	0
Jujube, 3 oz	65	0
Kiwifruit, 1 medium, 3 oz	45	0
1 large, 4 oz	60	0
Kumquats, 5 medium, 3 1/2 oz	60	0

	CALS	FAT
Kiwano, 1/2 medium, 5 oz	35	0
Langsat, duku, 1 medium, 2 oz	25	0
Lemon, 1 medium, 4 oz	20	0
1 wedge, 1 oz	5	0
Limes, 1 only, 2 oz	20	0
Loganberries, Frozen,		
1/2 cup, 2 1/2 oz	40	0
Logans, 5 fruit, 1/2 oz	10	0
Loquats, 4 fruit, 2 1/4 oz	20	0
Lychees, 4 fruit, 2 1/4 oz	25	0
Mamey Apple, 1 whole, 3 lb	430	4
1/4 fruit (1 cup flesh) 7 oz	100	1
Mandarin: I small, 3 oz	25	0
1 medium, 4 oz	35	0
1 large, 6 oz	55	0
Mango, fresh, 1/2 cup slice, 3 oz	55	0
1 whole medium, 11 oz	140	<1
Melons: Average all types		
1 cup, cubes/balls, 6 oz	60	0
Monstera Deliciosa (Taxonia),		
Edible part, 4 oz	50	0
Mulberries, 20 fruit, 1 oz	15	0
Nashi fruit (Asian Pear),		
1 medium, 4 1/2 oz	50	0
Nectarines, 1 medium, 4 oz	50	0
1 large, 5 1/2 oz	70	0
Oheloberries, 1/2 cup, 2 1/2 oz	20	0
Olives, Pickled:		
Green, 10 large, 1 1/2 oz	45	5
Ripe, Greek Style, 10 med 1 oz	70	7
Ripe (Black), Californian:		
1 Small/ Median	4	<1
1 Large/ Extra Large	6	<1
1 Jumbo	7	<1
1 Colossal	9	1
1 Super Colossal	13	1
Oranges, Average all varieties:		
1 Small, 5 oz	50	0
1 Medium, 8 oz	80	0
1 Large, 10 oz	95	0
Californian: Valencias, 8oz	85	0
Navels (thick skin) 8 oz	70	0
Flesh only, 1 cup, 6 oz	80	0
Florida, 1 Medium, 7 oz	70	0
Papaya, 1/2 cup, cubed, 2 1/2 oz	30	0
1 medium, 16 oz	120	<1
Passion fruit, 1 medium, 1 1/4 oz	20	0

	CALS	FAT
Peaches: 1 med (4 per lb). 4 oz	35	0
1 large, 6 oz	55	0
Pears: Bartlett, 1 small, 4 oz	60	0
1 medium, 6 oz	90	<1
1 Large, 8 oz	120	< 1
Bosc, 6 oz	90	<1
D'Anjou, 1 medium, 8 oz	120	<1
Red Pear, 5 oz	80	<1
Asian (Nashi), 1 large, 7 oz	80	0
Pepino, 1/2 medium, 4 oz	20	0
Persimmons: Native, 1 oz	30	0
Japan (2 1/2'd x 3 1/2'h), 7 oz	120	0
Seedless (Maui), 1 med., 5 oz	100	0
Pineapple (flesh only): 1 slice,		
(3/4 thick, 3 1/2" diam.), 3 oz	40	0
1 cup. Diced, 5 1/2 oz	80	1
1 medium, 4 1/2 lb	525	5
Pitanga, 3 fruit, 1 oz	6	0
Plantains, 1/2 cup slices. 2 1/2 oz	90	0
Plums, average all types		
Mini/Damson (1"dm.), 1/2 oz	8	0
Small (1 3/4" diam.), 1/2 oz	30	0
Medium (2 1/4" diam.). 3 oz	45	0
Large (2 1/2 diam.), 4 oz	65	0
Pomegranates, 1/2 fruit, 5 oz	55	0
Pummelo, fresh, 1/2 cup, 4 oz.	35	0
Prickly Pears, 1 fruit, 5 oz	40	<1
Quinces, 1 fruit, 5 oz	50	0
Rambutan (Rambotang),		
Red/ Yellow, 1 med., 2 oz	15	0
Raspberries, 1/2 cup, 2 oz	30	0
Rhubarb, raw, 1/2 cup, 2 oz	15	0
Sapodilla (chico), 1 med, 7 1/2 oz	140	2
Sapotes, 1 medium, 11 oz	300	1
Soursop, 1 cup pulp, 8 oz	150	<1
Strawberries: 1 cup, 5 1/2 oz	45	<1
6 medium/3 large, 2 oz	15	0
1 pint, 12 oz	95	1
Sugar Apples, 1/2 cup pulp, 4 oz	120	0
Tamarind: 1 fruit, 4 oz	5	0
Tangelo: 1 small, 4 oz	30	0
1 medium, 5 oz	40	0
1 Large, 7 oz	55	0
Tangerine, 1 fruit, 4 oz	35	0
Tangor, 1 medium, 4 oz	35	0
Tomato: Cherry, 1 med., 3/4 oz	5	0
1 Small, 3 oz	25	0
1 Medium, 5 oz	35	0

INDEX

INDEX

INDEX

Lewis SJ, Heaton KW. Increasing butyrate concentration in the distal colon by accelerating intestinal transit. Gut Aug. 1997;41(2):245-51.

Aldoori WH, Giovanucci EL, Rockett HR, Sampson L, Rimm EB, Willett WC. A Prospective study of dietary fiber types and symptomatic divertivular disease in men. J Nutr Apr 1998;128(4):714-9

Rimm EB, Ascherio A, Gioannucci E, Spiegelman D, Stampfer MJ, Willett WC. Vegetable, fruit, and cereal fiber intake and risk of coronary heart disease among Men.JAMA Feb 1996;275(6):447-51

Howe GR, Benito E, Castelleto R, Cornee J, Esteve J, Gallagher RP, Iscovich JM, Dengao J, Kaaks R, Kune GA, et al. Dietary intake of fiber and decreased risk of cancers of the colon and rectum: evidence from the combined analysis of 13 case-controlled studies. J Natl Canc Inst Dec 1992;84(24):187-96.

Turcoatte LP, Hespal PJ, Graham TE, Richter EA. Impaired plasma FFA oxidation imposed by extreme CHO deficiency in contracting rat skeletal muscle. J Appl Physiol. Aug 1994;77(2):517-25.

Sahlin K, Katz A, Broberg S. Tricarboxyclic acid cycle intermediates in human muscle During prolonged exercise.AM J Physiol Nov 1990;259(5 Pt. L):C834-41.

Karlsson J, Saltin B. Lactate ATP, and CP in working muscles during exhaustive exercise in man. J Appl Physiol Nov 1970;29(5):596-602

Shick SM, Wing RR, Klem ML, McGuire MT, Hill JO, Seagle H. Persons successful at long-term weight loss and maintenance continue to consume a low-energy, low fat diet. J AM Diet Assoc Apr 1998;98(4):408-13

McDowell MA, Briefel RR, Alaimo K, Bischof AM, Caughman CR, Carroll MD, Loria CM, Johnson CL. Energy intakes of persons ages 2 months and over in the United States: third national health and nutrition examination survey, phase 1, 1998-91. Adv Data Oct 1994;24(255):1-24.

US Department of Health and Human Services. Physical activity and health: a report of the surgeon General. Atlanta, GA: Centers for Disease Control and Prevention; 1996.

Groff JL, Gropper SS, Hunt SM. Advanced nutrition and human metabolism. St. Paul, MN: West Publishing Company; 1995. 575p.

Simopoulos AP. Omega-3 fatty acids in health and disease and in growth and development. AM J Clin Nutr Sep 1991;54(3):438-63

Simopoulos AP. Omega-3 fatty acids in the prevention-management of cardiovascular disease. Can J Physiol Pharmacol Mar 1997;75(3):234-9.

Lissner L, Levitsky DA, Strupp BJ, Kalkwarf HJ, Roe DA. Dietary fat and the regulation of energy intake in human subjects. AM J Clin Nutr Dec 1987;46(6):886-92

Lissner L, Heitmann BL. The dietary fat: carbohydrate ratio in relation to body Weight. Curr Opin Lipidol Feb 1995;6(1):8-13

Horton TJ, Drougas H, Reed GW, Peters JC, Hill JO. Fat and carbohydrate Overfeeding in humans: different effects on energy storage. Am J Clin Nutr Jul 1995;62(1):19-29.

American Diabetes Association. (2003). The diabetes assistance & resources (DAR) program.

American Heart Association. (2002). Heart disease and stroke statistics—2003

American Heart Association. (2003). Hispanics and cardiovascular disease.

Centers for Disease Control and Prevention (CDC). (1998, last reviewed April 2003). Hispanics and tobacco. Atlanta, GA: CDC.

Centers for Disease Control and Prevention (CDC). (2002). Obesity still on the rise, new data show.

Webster's ninth new collegiate dictionary. Springfield, MA: Merriam-Webster Inc.;1991. 1564 p.

Position of the American Dietetic Association: weight management. J Am Diet Assoc Jan 1997;97(1):71-4

Faires VM. Thermodynamics. New York: Macmillan Company;1967.

Jensen, MD. Diet effects on fatty acid metabolism in lean and obese humans. AM J Clin Nutr 1998(68 suppl):531-4.

Agricultural Research Service. Fat intake continues to drop; veggies, fruit still low in the US diet. Res News 1996.

Shils ME, Young VR.Modern Nutrition in health and disease.7thedition. Philadelphia,PA: Lea & Febiger; 1988.pp.1694.

Tarnopolsky MA, Atkinson SA, MacDougall JD, Chesley A, Phillip S, Schwarcz HP. Evaluation of protein requirements for trained strength athletes. J Appl Phys 1992;73(2):767-75.

Lemon PW, Tarnopolsky MA, MacDougall JD, Atkinson SA. Protein requirements and muscle mass/strength changes during intensive training in novice body builders. J Appl Phys 1992;73(2):767-75.

Kuel J. The relationship between circulation and metabolism during exercise.Med Sci Sports 1973;5:209.

Keul J, Doll E. Keppler D. Energy metabolism of human muscle. Baltimore, MD: University Park; 1972.

Roy B, Tarnopolsky M, MacDougall J, Fowles J, Yarasheski K. Effect of glucose Supplement timing on protein metabolism after resistance training. J Appl Physiol Jun 1997;82(6):1882-8.

Smolin LA, Grosvenor MB. Nutrition science and applications. Orlando, FL: Saunders College Publishing; 1994.pp.576.

Rolls BJ, Hill JO. Carbohydrate and weight management. Washington, DC: ILSI Press 1998.pp.60.

Jenkins DJ, Vuksan V, Kendall CW, Wursch P, Jeffcoat R, Waring S, Mehling CC Vidgen E, Augustin LS, Wong E. Physiological effects of resistant starches on fecal bulk, short chain fatty acids, blood lipids and glycemic index. J AM Coll Nutr Dec 1198; 17(6):609-16.

Centers for Disease Control and Prevention (CDC). (2003). National health and nutrition examination survey: Cholesterol status among adults in the United States.

The Provider's Guide to Quality & Culture

Centers for Disease Control and Prevention (CDC). (2003). Obesity trends: 1991–2001. prevalence of obesity among US adults, by characteristics.

Hoffman, C., and Pohl, M. (2000). Health insurance coverage in America: 1999 data update.

Washington, DC: Kaiser Commission on Medicaid and the Uninsured. Hong, B., and Bayat, N. (1999). National Asian American and Pacific Islander cardio vascular health action plan: Eliminating racial and ethnic disparities in cardiovascular health: Improving the cardiovascular health of Asian American and Pacific Islander populations in the United States.

Kaiser Permanente. (2001). A provider's handbook on culturally competent care: Latino population. Oakland, CA: Kaiser Permanente National Diversity Council.

National Diabetes Information Clearinghouse. (2002). Diabetes in Hispanic Americans. NIH Publication No. 02-3265. Bethesda, MD: National Institute of Diabetes
and Digestive and Kidney Diseases (NIDDK), National Institutes of Health.

National Women's American/Latino women. Washington, DC: US DHHS, Office on Women's Health. Health Information Center. (2003). Frequently asked questions about health problems in Hispanic

Oldways Preservation and Exchange Trust. (2003). The Latin American diet pyramid.

Pleis, F.R., and Coles, R. (2002). Summary health statistics for US adults: National health interview survey, 1998. Vital Health Statistics 10(209). Atlanta, GA: National Center for Health Statistics.

smedley, B.D., Stith, A.Y., and Nelson, A.R. (eds.). (2003). Unequal treatment: Confronting racial and ethnic disparities in health care. Washington, DC:

National Academies Press, Institute of Medicine of the National Academies.

Talamantes, M., Lindeman, R., and Mouton, C. (2003). Ethnogeriatric curriculum module: Health and health care of Hispanic/Latino American elders. Stanford University.

Tamir, A., and Cachola, S. (1994). Hypertension and other cardiovascular risk factors. In Zane, N.W.S., Takeuchi, D.T., and Young, K.N.J. (eds.). Confronting critical health issues of Asian and Pacific Islander Americans. Thousand Oaks, CA: Sage, pp. 209–246.

US Department of Health and Human Services (US DHHS). (2000). Healthy people 2010: Understanding and improving health, 2nd ed. Washington, DC: US Government Printing Office.

US Department of Health and Human Services (US DHHS). (2003).

Demographics and health disparities. Draft curriculum module 2 for Cultural Competence in the Clinical Care Model Project. Health Resources and Services Administration, Bureau of Primary Health Care.

Department of Health. Nutritional Aspects of Cardiovascular Disease. HMSO. 1994

Department of Health. Dietary Reference Values for Food Energy and Nutrients for the United Kingdom. HMSO. 1991.

www.foodsubs.com

www.fishermansexpress.com

www.chili-pepper-plants.com

November 24th 2003 - Cinnamon significantly reduces blood sugar levels in diabetics, by Richard Anderson at the US Department of Agriculture's Human Nutrition Research Center in Beltsville, Maryland.

The American Heritage Dictionary of the English Language, Fourth Edition

American Institute for Cancer Research at 1-800-843-8114 or visit their website at www.aicr.org.· Cholesterol, and Coronary Heart Disease, #71-1019 Circulation. 1990;81:1721-1733

AHA Scientific Statement: Guidelines for Weight Management Programs for Healthy Adults, #71-0053 Heart Disease and Stroke. 1994;3:221-228

AHA Scientific Statement: Trans Fatty Acids, Lipids, and Risk of Developing Cardiovascular Disease, #71-0116 Circulation. 1997;95:2588-2590

AHA Science Advisory: Obesity and Heart Disease, #71-0130 Circulation. 1997;96:3248-3250

AHA Scientific Statement: Very Low Fat Diets, #71-0143 Circulation. 1998;98:935-939

AHA Scientific Statement: AHA Dietary Guidelines: Revision 2000, #71-0193 Circulation. 2000;102:2284-2299; Stroke. 2000;31:2751-2766

AHA Conference Proceedings: Summary of the Scientific Conference on Dietary Fatty Acids and Cardiovascular Health, #71-0200 Circulation. 2001;103:1034-1039

AHA Science Advisory: Lyon Diet Heart Study: Benefits of a Mediterranean-Style, National Cholesterol Education Program/American Heart Association Step
I Dietary Pattern on Cardiovascular Disease, #71-0202 Circulation. 2001;103:1823-1825; Editorial: Can a Mediterranean-Style Diet Reduce Heart Disease? Circulation. 2001;103:1821-1822